a practical guide to VAT

FOR charities AND voluntary organisations

▼ KATE SAYER ▼

DIRECTORY OF SOCIAL CHANGE

Published by

The Directory of Social Change
24 Stephenson Way
London NW1 2DP
tel: 020 7209 5151, fax: 020 7209 5049
e-mail: info@dsc.org.uk
from whom further copies and a full publications list are available.

The Directory of Social Change is a Registered Charity no. 800517

Copyright © Directory of Social Change 2001

The moral right of the author has been asserted in accordance with the Copyright, Designs and Patents Act 1988.

All rights reserved. No part of this book may be stored in a retrieval system or reproduced in any form whatsoever without prior permission in writing from the publisher. This book is sold subject to the condition that it shall not, by way of trade or otherwise, be lent, re-sold, hired out or otherwise circulated without the publisher's prior permission in any form of binding or cover other than that in which it is published, and without a similar condition including this condition being imposed on the subsequent purchaser.

ISBN 1 900360 62 4

British Library Cataloguing in Publication Data
A catalogue record for this book is available from the British Library

Designed and typeset by Penny Drinkwater
Cover design by Penny Drinkwater

Printed and bound by Page Bros, Norwich

Other Directory of Social Change departments in London:
Courses and Conferences tel: 020 7209 4949
Charity Centre tel: 020 7209 1015
Research tel: 020 7209 4422
Finance and Administration tel: 020 7209 0902

Directory of Social Change Northern Office:
Federation House, Hope Street,
Liverpool L1 9BW
Courses and Conferences tel: 0151 708 0117
Research tel: 0151 708 0136

Acknowledgements

The genesis of this book goes back a long way – to simple one-day courses at the Directory of Social Change which sought to explain VAT to charity staff and trustees. Based on those courses, I wrote the first edition of *A Practical Guide to VAT for Charities* in response to a huge demand for something that would simplify VAT for charities. This new edition goes a little further and covers more of the experience of charities since that early book. I am grateful to all the people who have attended courses and seminars and to all our clients, as it is through your questions that I have learnt.

I am grateful to Alison Baxter at the Directory of Social Change for her support and patience, needed more than ever for this edition as finding the time to research and write was more difficult than ever. I owe an enormous debt of gratitude to Tony Martin who helped me to find that time and supports me in all my work. Thanks also to Liz Rosser at Sayer Vincent who particularly contributed to the content and to all the team at Sayer Vincent who also contributed ideas and experience.

CONTENTS

Introduction   5
• What this book covers and who it is for. • Overall context – why VAT is a problem for charities.

1 What is VAT?   8
• Basics of VAT and how it works as a tax. • Glossary. • How VAT works for businesses. • Example showing effect of prices including or excluding VAT.

2 When do you have to register for VAT?   12
• Rules of registration and requirement to register. • Compulsory registration, voluntary registration. • Recovering pre-registration VAT on purchases. • Penalties for late registration. • Exemption from registration. • Branches. • De-registration. • Case study – assessing income to decide when to register.

3 Activities of charities   21
• Establishing the VAT category for the various activities undertaken by charities in pursuing their charitable objects. • Non-business activities, contracts, membership subscriptions, and apportioning benefits. • Exempt activities. • Education, vocational training, funded training courses, New Deal, youth clubs, research and other educational supplies. • Health and welfare, exempt welfare services, registered homes and other care services. • Subscriptions to professional bodies. • Sporting activities. • Cultural services. • Zero-rated activities. • Standard-rated activities.

4 Fundraising   39
• VAT on different types of fundraising income, including collecting donations, sponsorship, cause-related marketing. • Fundraising events, challenge events, lotteries, sale of donated goods, gifts in kind and other.

5 Recovering VAT   49
• Recovering VAT on business activities, identifying the recoverable VAT. • Partial exemption rules and examples of where VAT fully recoverable and only partly recoverable. • Annual adjustment. • Charities with non-business and exempt activities. • Standard method of apportioning residual VAT, special methods. • Provisional recovery rate.

6 Saving VAT   61
• Nature of relief and when available. • Goods and services eligible, including advertising, aids for disabled people, collecting tins and badges, medical equipment, vehicles, printed matter and other.

3

A PRACTICAL GUIDE TO VAT

7 *International aspects of VAT* *75*

• VAT applicable to services, exports and imports. • Reliefs available to charities.
• Transactions within the European Community, buying from the EC, distance selling.
• Registering for VAT in other EC countries; recovering VAT on purchases from other
EC countries.

8 *Property* *82*

• Undertaking new construction and obtaining zero rates. • Refurbishing and
extending buildings, including listed buildings. • Renting out property as landlords.
• Occupying property as tenants.

9 *Planning for VAT* *94*

• Typical VAT problems in charities and strategies to overcome them. • Simple ideas
for planning VAT, including membership, admission charges, postage and packing.
• Group registration, branches. • Education and welfare on a 'for-profit' basis.
• Fundraising events. • Charging for staff time and services. • Grants as a subsidy for
business activities.

10 *Operational aspects* *102*

• Registering for VAT, issuing VAT invoices, keeping records and bookkeeping.
• Completing a VAT return and proper VAT accounting. • Records to be maintained.
• Mileage allowances, pre-registration purchases. • Cash accounting and annual
accounting. • Retail schemes, bad debt relief, late submission of VAT returns.
• Dealing with Customs & Excise, declaring errors, interest and penalties. • Appendix
with guide to using Sage codes for bookkeeping when VAT registered.

Summaries of useful VAT cases *115*

Further information *121*

Index *124*

INTRODUCTION

This book attempts to provide an explanation for non-specialists in charities of how VAT operates. Chapter 10 on *Operational aspects* is written for those who have no knowledge or experience of VAT, whereas chapter 9 on *Planning* does assume existing knowledge and at least a working knowledge of chapters 3 to 6. VAT is a complex tax and it is therefore not possible to cover every aspect of the VAT rules in a short guide. VAT is governed by laws and just as other aspects of the law change or may be challenged, so it is with VAT. There are new cases and new interpretations arising all the time and so sometimes the current view of a particular area will be different to the accepted treatment of some years ago. Readers should therefore get up-to-date advice before acting.

This book covers the law and cases up to October 2000. You will find updates on the Sayer Vincent website: www.sayervincent.co.uk

Charities enjoy tax exempt status for all types of income tax, providing the income is applied for charitable purposes and does not arise from a purely commercial trading activity. There is no such tax exempt status when it comes to VAT. There are some special situations when charities do not have to pay VAT, but these are quite specific to certain categories and items. Otherwise, charities have to comply with the VAT rules in just the same way as any other enterprise.

This particularly applies to charities when they are undertaking activities such as fundraising or other trading activities. You have to look at the activity itself and apply the normal VAT rules to the activity. A crucial part of this book looks at the different activities charities typically undertake and how the VAT rules apply to them. VAT planning is possible where the charity can arrange its activities in such a way that it fits a particular set of rules.

Charities pay a great deal of tax on their purchases. The Charities' Tax Reform Group has estimated that charities spend £400 million in VAT annually. It had been hoped that the Review of Charity Taxation announced by the Chancellor in July 1997 would relieve this burden. The main objective of the review had been to look at the way that VAT applied to charities and to simplify the administration of VAT. The final outcome of the review has barely touched on VAT and focuses mainly on tax-effective giving. Whilst it is possible that the charity sector as a whole will benefit from improvements to the tax regime for donations, this will not always be evenly spread. Many charities providing services pay VAT on the goods and services they buy in, with no chance of recovering that VAT. These same charities may not be raising funds from the public and so will not gain from improvements to tax-effective giving.

The system has not really been simplified, although there are a few welcome changes to the rules which will make it easier for charities. However, charities will still face some uncertainty as to how the rules apply in individual situations and the calculations for estimating the amount of VAT recoverable in a VAT registered charity are still complex.

This is mainly because VAT is a complex tax which is part of the European Community (EC) tax system, and the rules stem from the EC, not the British Parliament. We can look forward to many changes in this tax as a single market in Europe develops. We already have a minimum rate of VAT of 5% across Europe, so any changes reflect this rate. The zero rate of VAT applicable to many supplies in the UK can be retained for the time being, but a major review of VAT is underway in Europe, moving towards a definitive system across the EC. The harmonisation of the scope of the tax is also on the agenda. Although it may seem that none of this has anything to do with charities, it will inevitably affect them. The key point to watch will be the rates of tax applied to certain categories of items. For example, charity advertising is currently at zero rate in the UK. This is not the case in other EC countries and we may have to change the rate in order to come into line. Other examples exist in the range of concessions offered to charities in the UK, many of which are not available elsewhere in Europe.

Charities in the UK should involve themselves in the work of lobbying groups, such as the Charities' Tax Reform Group. There is a great danger that the charity perspective will be lost in Europe. The UK has a much larger charity and voluntary sector than any other EC country. Charity interests in matters such as VAT need to be pressed home.

Charities are often complex organisations with many different activities. Their VAT situation may, therefore, be complex. Various aspects are examined in detail in the rest of this book. There are, however, some important points which should be borne in mind when considering an organisation's VAT position.

▼ An organisation will not necessarily be worse off or better off if it has to register for VAT.

▼ It is important to look at the overall picture, not at particular activities in isolation.

▼ Consider who your consumers are and what their VAT position is. They may be able to reclaim all the VAT you charge, or it may effectively increase your prices.

▼ A lot of the input VAT you have paid on your purchases may be recoverable, if your affairs are arranged to be tax efficient from the point of view of VAT.

▼ Organisations which are mainly service providers (where their main costs are wages) are likely to have little input VAT to recover, but if they register for VAT will have to charge VAT on their labour.

▼ Registration for VAT is not optional. It is a matter of fact and law as to whether an organisation or person should register for VAT or not and there are several penalties for non-registration.

It is therefore important that charities obtain proper advice before committing themselves to a course of action. It is always important to see VAT as one of the considerations you should take into account when deciding how to plan your activities. Direct tax, charity law, the charity's objects and strategic direction all have to be taken into consideration.

However, it is hoped that this book will give many trustees and staff clear pointers so that they can inform themselves more fully of the VAT rules.

1 ▾ What is VAT?

This chapter provides a basic introduction for those not familiar with VAT, explaining the language used and the practical operation of the tax in daily life. Further information about bookkeeping and issuing invoices is given in chapter 10 *Operational aspects.*

Value Added Tax (VAT) is a sales tax paid by the purchaser or consumer and collected by HM Customs & Excise. It is included in the price that the end consumer pays for most everyday items. There are certain exceptions, such as basic foodstuffs, books, certain printed matter and children's clothing.

Goods and services are divided into different categories, which determine whether VAT should be charged on them or not. The categories are:

▾ standard;

▾ zero;

▾ exempt;

▾ outside the scope (non-business).

Most goods and services are subject to VAT at standard rate. The VAT legislation lists in detail the goods and services which are exempt or zero-rated.

'Supplies' is the term used in VAT guidance to describe the goods and services supplied by an organisation to bring in income. It will include straightforward sales for an income earning project; it will also include rent, interest, grants, donations. It really means all the activities of an organisation.

'Taxable' has a specific meaning when talking about VAT. Taxable supplies are the activities which fall into the categories of standard-rated and zero-rated. A 'taxable person' is someone who should register for VAT.

'Outside the scope' describes some activities which are determined to be 'non-business'. These are activities such as private transactions between individuals, including employment. It also encompasses a lot of charitable and voluntary activity.

'Business' activities, on the other hand, are any commercial activity. For a business transaction to exist, there must be a supply of goods or services for a reasonable price ('consideration'). Hence selling cups of coffee at a price which at least covers the cost of ingredients is considered a business transaction, whereas a charity which gives away coffee is doing something which is outside the scope.

GLOSSARY OF VAT TERMINOLOGY

▼ **Business activities**

Defined by VAT law as the exchange of goods or services for value.

▼ **Non-business activities**

Supplies made with no commercial intent, such as voluntary donations.

▼ **Outside the scope**

Certain activities are not covered by the VAT regime, principally employment (salaries are not subject to VAT) and non-business transactions.

▼ **Exempt**

Certain business activities do not carry any VAT because they are on a list of exempt goods or services, e.g. health services.

▼ **Taxable**

The two categories of zero-rated and standard-rated come under a group of taxable activities.

▼ **Zero-rated**

Certain business activities are taxable, but carry VAT at zero-rate.

▼ **Standard-rated**

VAT must be charged by VAT-registered businesses at 17.5% (currently).

▼ **Reduced-rate**

Certain supplies carry VAT at a reduced rate of 5%, such as fuel and power.

▼ **Input VAT**

The VAT on business purchases which may be recovered by being offset against output VAT.

▼ **Output VAT**

The VAT you charge on sales and which you have to collect from customers. You then pay this over to Customs & Excise (after deducting input VAT you have paid out on purchases).

See also the diagram at the beginning of chapter 3, p21.

HOW VAT WORKS FOR BUSINESSES

All businesses with a certain turnover have to register for VAT, which means that they have to charge VAT on the goods and services they supply (output VAT). They are also buying in goods and services in the course of their business which carry VAT (input VAT). All transactions are therefore bought and sold including VAT.

Each registered business has to keep records showing the value of each transaction and the amount of VAT included. At the end of each quarter, the totals of output VAT and input VAT have to be entered onto a return. The difference between the two has to be made up. If the amount of output VAT is the greater, which is usually the case, then the business pays the difference over to Customs & Excise. Effectively the business is charging and collecting tax on the government's behalf. If the amount of input VAT is the greater, then this amount will be repaid to the business.

If a business is registered for VAT, the VAT on purchases does not cost the business anything, as it can all be recovered a little later through the offset against the VAT charged on sales on the VAT return. The output VAT charged on sales is not income to the trader, as this will have to be remitted to Customs & Excise. The trader is simply collecting the tax on behalf of the government. In the following example, the person who bought the dining chairs, however, has had to pay £470 – the trader's selling price plus the VAT. As a private individual, or an enterprise not registered for VAT, there is no recovery of VAT and so the full cost to them is the whole amount paid.

How VAT works

Woodworks Limited manufacture chairs. They have the following transactions in their books:

Purchase of wood	£117.50
VAT included	£17.50
Goods value	£100.00

VAT is charged at 17.5% on the value of goods, in this case £100. Woodworks pays a total of £117.50.

After manufacturing the chairs, they are sold at £400 plus VAT at 17.5%. The total VAT paid by the purchaser of the chairs is £70.

Sale of chairs - selling price	£470.00
VAT included	£70.00
Goods value	£400.00

Woodwork Ltd will show on its VAT return:

Output VAT	£70.00
Input VAT	£17.50
Net payable to Customs & Excise	£52.50

Assuming that both these transactions have occurred in the same accounting period, Woodworks pays Customs & Excise £52.50. This is the amount of VAT it has collected, less the amount it has paid on its purchases.

The amount of VAT payable is the tax due on the value added because the wood has been converted into a set of dining chairs.

Check:

Value of goods sold	£400.00
Value of goods bought	£100.00
Difference, i.e. value added	£300.00
VAT thereon @ 17.5%	£52.50

The income and expenditure of a trader registered for VAT is therefore all stated at the values excluding VAT. The VAT makes no difference to the profit or loss of the enterprise.

It may make a difference to pricing, however. To illustrate this point, consider the situation of Jane, who is a freelance consultant. Currently, her turnover is below the VAT threshold and so she does not have to charge VAT. If she is successful, she may consider expanding the business by taking on an employee. The increased turnover would lead to VAT registration and then she would have to add VAT to her fees. This would make her more expensive to her clients. She would not be recovering much VAT on costs, as her principal costs are labour. She may even have to reduce her prices to remain competitive.

Organisations and businesses which are not registered for VAT may not charge or recover any of the VAT on their costs. Unregistered organisations therefore have to budget for all costs including VAT.

Hence VAT can be a cost to an organisation. However, it is never a simple matter of registering and charging VAT so that you can recover all the VAT on purchases. You have to be undertaking business activities, and then you can only recover VAT on your business activities. There is quite a lot of administration and bookkeeping involved and, as the example of Jane demonstrated, VAT may in fact increase your prices.

2 ▼ When do you have to register for VAT?

This chapter explains the registration rules and the requirement to register. It also gives practical examples of how to apply the rules and looks at situations where charities may need to plan carefully, for example if they have branches.

An individual or an organisation has to register for VAT and therefore start charging VAT on all sales of goods or services once the value of those sales goes over the registration threshold (£52,000 since 1 April 2000). This is easily established for ordinary businesses, but can be more complicated for charities as you first have to check which income-generating activities would count as 'sales' in the context of VAT.

VAT guidance notes talk about 'supplies', which means most forms of income. However, it can also mean an activity which does not actually produce an income. So, for example, certain charities provide a free advice service, or give away soup to the homeless. This is still a 'supply' in VAT terms, although not a taxable supply.

'Taxable' also has a specific meaning in VAT. It means goods or services provided which are liable to VAT either at the standard rate or at the zero rate when the goods are supplied by a trader registered for VAT.

Some activities are outside the scope of VAT altogether. This includes individuals working in an employment: you do not have to send your employer a VAT invoice if you earn over the VAT registration threshold. It also includes all transactions between private individuals not in business, and it also includes charitable donations.

Some goods and services are exempt from VAT, whoever buys and sells them. The exemption has to be given through legislation and the categories of goods and services are listed in VAT leaflets.

So, first this chapter describes the rules for VAT registration. The next step to answering the question 'When do you have to register for VAT?' is to draw up a list of your organisation's activities and sources of income. Then check which category the activity falls into. The categories of VAT applying to the activities of charities and fundraising by charities is covered in greater depth in other chapters.

You will need to determine the following.

▼ Is the activity business or non-business (outside the scope)?

▼ If business, is it exempt or taxable (including both standard-rated and zero-rated supplies)?

▼ Is the taxable income sufficiently high that you are required to register for VAT?

REQUIREMENT TO REGISTER

You are required to register if:

▼ at the end of any month, the value of taxable supplies in the past 12 months has exceeded the *annual threshold*; or

▼ at any time, there are reasonable grounds for believing that the value of taxable supplies in the next 30 days will exceed the annual threshold.

There is one month in which to register. You should register by obtaining and completing a VAT registration form. On the form, you must give a date from which you will charge VAT. From then onwards you must provide and keep proper VAT invoices. Quarterly returns will be sent automatically and must be completed and returned within one month of the end of the quarter.

This is *compulsory* registration. Note that registration has no retrospective effect if you register on time. It is a 'trigger' for registering and charging VAT in future. Note also how the 12-month period operates; this does not refer to your financial year or the tax year. It is the past 12 months going back from the current month. If you are close to the threshold, therefore, you need to set up a system for monitoring a rolling 12-month period, adding on the most recent month and deducting the earlier month. It is quite possible to receive a large new source of taxable income in one month which would take the organisation over the threshold and trigger registration. There is no need for apportionment; VAT will just apply to future invoices issued after registration.

A PRACTICAL GUIDE TO VAT

Example: Compulsory registration

People's Legal Advice has been providing free advice to members of the public for many years, receiving grants and donations to support this work. It has now been successful in a bid to provide advice to the residents of a housing association (a taxable supply) for a fee of £60,000. The fee is payable in four quarterly instalments:

	Invoice issued	Amount	Cumulative
Quarter 1	25 April	£15,000	£15,000
Quarter 2	25 July	£15,000	£30,000
Quarter 3	25 Oct	£15,000	£45,000
Quarter 4	25 Jan	£15,000	£60,000

The threshold is only exceeded retrospectively after the fourth quarter invoice is issued. Compulsory registration would be triggered at this point. People's Legal Advice would become liable to register on 31 January. They would need to inform Customs & Excise by 28 February and registration would be effective from 1 March. If the contract is not going to be renewed, then the organisation could request an exemption from registration on the grounds that future supplies will not exceed the registration threshold. Permission should be sought to do this, however, rather than acting unilaterally.

There is also an argument that the organisation knew that the threshold was going to be exceeded within 30 days at the beginning of January, as they knew they would be issuing a further invoice at the end of January. Customs & Excise should, in that case, have been notified by the end of January of liability from 1 January. In this instance, registration would take effect from 1 January.

Voluntary registration would also have been possible at the beginning of the contract (see next section).

VOLUNTARY REGISTRATION

You may wish to register for VAT even if the level of your taxable supplies does not reach the threshold. The advantages are that you may be able to recover some VAT on costs, and that you can operate one bookkeeping system right from the beginning of a new business in which you anticipate that registration will be necessary at some future date. You have to write a letter with your completed registration form explaining the nature of your business, why you want to be registered and from what date. Customs & Excise will need to be sure that you intend to carry on a business for VAT purposes, and so may request evidence such as contracts, copy invoices showing investment for new activity or other appropriate evidence. Note that any repayment of VAT on purchases in the first year is provisional; you may have to make a payment to Customs & Excise if you do not make any taxable supplies.

Your registration can be cancelled if your taxable supplies drop below the de-registration limit (£50,000 since 1 April 2000).

> ### *Example: Voluntary registration*
>
> ▼ The Dickens Charity provides free meals to the homeless. It receives grants and donations of approximately £200,000 per year for this work. It has also started to provide consultancy and advice to local authorities in other areas on ways in which such schemes can be established. They estimate that they will earn about £30,000 from this source.
>
> ▼ This organisation can apply for voluntary registration, once it starts the new consultancy service. (Before this, it could not even apply for voluntary registration, as it had no business activities at all.) VAT would have to be charged on the invoices for the consultancy services only. The charity would have to keep detailed records of its costs as well, and ensure that it identified which related to the consultancy activity. The input VAT on purchases which related to the consultancy could be reclaimed, but not all the VAT on all activities.

RECOVERING PRE-REGISTRATION VAT ON PURCHASES

It is possible to recover VAT that has been incurred prior to the date of registration by making a claim on the first VAT return under the category of input tax. Goods that have been purchased for the purpose of the business and are still 'on-hand' at the date of registration either as fixed assets or stock are eligible for the VAT recovery, providing they were not purchased more than three years prior to registration. Services supplied up to six months prior to the date of registration are eligible for the recovery.

PENALTIES FOR LATE REGISTRATION

If your taxable supplies exceed the annual registration threshold and you do not take action to register for VAT, then you will have to account for the VAT which should have been charged and pay a penalty. The penalty will depend on how late the registration is:

▼ 9 months or less   5% of tax payable
▼ More than 9 months but less than 18 months   10% of tax payable
▼ Over 18 months   15% of tax payable

Where the amounts as calculated above are small, or you are in fact due a repayment from Customs & Excise as a result of registering, a minimum penalty of £50 applies.

Note that there is a limit of three years on all claims, so a registration cannot be back-dated more than three years.

The VAT has to be calculated and paid over as if you had registered on time. This VAT may not be recoverable from your customers. So, you may have to go through the taxable income and assume that the amount you received included VAT at the appropriate rate. You would then have to calculate the VAT included using the formula:

$$\frac{\text{VAT inclusive amount} \times 17.5}{117.5}$$

You will be able to recover the VAT on purchases that relate directly or indirectly to the taxable activity, so this will offset the amount finally due to the VAT office.

Example: Late registration

▼ The Health Promotion Trust received £65,000 from a company to fund research and to publish the results. They treated this as a donation and later discovered that it should have been treated as advertising, since the company received considerable promotion from the deal. This is their only taxable supply in the year. This income on its own exceeds the threshold for registration and VAT must be accounted for. The company has refused to accept a late invoice adding the VAT, so they will have to treat the amount received as the VAT inclusive amount.

Calculation:

$$\frac{£65,000 \times 17.5}{117.5} = £9,680.85$$

▼ So, £9,680.85 will have to be remitted to Customs & Excise in VAT. The net income to the Health Promotion Trust is now only £55,319.15. If they had registered in time and agreed the arrangement with the company, then they would have issued an invoice for £65,000 plus VAT of £11,375. They would have paid the VAT over to Customs & Excise, but would have had £65,000 of income.

▼ They can also go through their purchase records to establish VAT on costs relating to the taxable activity as well as a proportion of shared costs, thus reducing the liability to the VAT office.

▼ This example also underlines the need for careful wording in contracts. Had there been a clause in the contract (or exchange of letters) stating that all fees payable would be subject to VAT where applicable, then the trust would have been able to issue a late invoice. However, the omission of such a clause means that the company was allowed to say that the amount paid included VAT.

EXEMPTION FROM REGISTRATION

It may be possible to apply to Customs & Excise requesting exemption from registration. This is not necessary if your only income is either outside the scope or exempt, or if taxable supplies are below the registration threshold. In addition, exceptional items such as the sale of capital equipment will not trigger registration. Application for exemption from registration is necessary if you have exceeded or will exceed the registration threshold, but the majority of your taxable supplies are zero-rated. Customs & Excise will normally grant the exemption where the tax recoverable would consistently exceed the tax payable. You must monitor the balance of your activities and notify Customs & Excise as soon as there is a material change.

Example: Exemption from registration

▼ The Legal Advice Trust publishes books and sends a newsletter to subscribers. It derives all its income from these activities. In 2000/01 they estimate that their income from these sources will reach £55,000.

▼ Income from publishing books and newsletters is zero-rated and therefore they will have taxable supplies in excess of £52,000. They should monitor their monthly income and should plan to register. Alternatively, they could submit the VAT registration form explaining that their only turnover is zero-rated and that they wish to be exempted from registration.

▼ Whilst avoidance of registration in this way keeps the bookkeeping simple, it does mean that they are unable to recover input VAT on overheads such as telephone and stationery. Recovery of this input VAT is only possible if you register for VAT. The trust should therefore compare the costs of registration (bookkeeping and administration costs) to the likely savings on recovered overheads when deciding whether or not to apply for exemption.

BRANCHES

Some charities have branches and local offices. The VAT legislation states that a *taxable person* must be registered for VAT. This can include any type of corporate body or individual. If a charity has branches which are under the control of the main office, then these should be included in one registration. You would have to look at their taxable supplies as well when considering whether the charity as a whole has gone over the threshold for registration.

You may have to consider totally autonomous branches for registration in their own right. This may be especially true for branches that are active in fundraising. Each branch would have to have sufficient turnover to exceed the threshold on its own. Each branch would have its own VAT registration number and would have to prepare and submit VAT returns. For this to apply, however, the branches must be quite autonomous. The constitution would have to be quite clear that the branch is separate and this would have to be borne out in practice. Customs & Excise would look for evidence that the branch had its own management, such as an independent management committee, and was responsible for its own financial and legal affairs.

Care is also needed in this area where there is a 'Friends of…' organisation in existence alongside a charity. Frequently the 'Friends' undertake considerable fundraising, although without the knowledge of the main charity. A clear decision needs to be made as to whether the 'Friends' should be separately constituted and accountable for its own affairs.

There should be no attempt to artificially split up activities just to avoid registration. The penalties for non-registration are high if it is later shown that the organisation should have been considered as a whole. Properly constituted separate branches or trading companies, on the other hand, are quite legal.

Example: Branches

▼ The Children's Welfare Association has a head office in Manchester and branches all over Lancashire. Several of the branches run charity shops selling donated goods and they remitted £30,000 of profits to head office. Head office produced a book on social policy last year, which resulted in royalties of £5,000.

▼ Further investigation reveals that the gross income of the charity shops was £50,000 before deduction of rent and service costs. This is zero-rated income. Royalties are standard-rated. Together they amount to £55,000 of taxable supplies. The charity should register for VAT or seek exemption from registration.

DE-REGISTRATION

If your turnover falls below a certain limit (£50,000 since 1 April 2000), then you can ask for registration to be cancelled. You would have to be able to explain why you thought that the taxable supplies would drop below the threshold in the forthcoming year. Upon de-registration, you will have to account for VAT on assets and stock held, unless no input VAT was reclaimed when the item was first purchased. This will be the case, for example, for a car. For fixed assets, an allowance will be made for depreciation.

Your registration can also be cancelled if the VAT office consider that you should no longer be registered. This would be the case if you had been submitting returns for a year or more showing little taxable activity.

It is important that charities are not complacent about the need to register for VAT. A small change in activities could take them over the threshold. Higher income from a particular source could tip the scales. Charities will also need to keep VAT in mind when they plan future activities, particularly where this involves expansion, significant changes and new ways of fundraising.

Example: When to register for VAT

Do-Good Charity is concerned that they should be registered for VAT. They have prepared an extract from their accounts to show the sources of income.

Donations	£30,000
Shop selling donated goods	£24,000
Flag day	£20,000
Grants	£18,000
Christmas cards	£12,000
Publications	£10,000
Advertising in magazine	£8,000
Bank interest	£4,500
Total income	**£126,500**

Step 1 *Go through the sources of income and categorise them for VAT purposes.*

Donations	£30,000	outside the scope
Shop selling donated goods	£24,000	zero-rated
Flag day	£20,000	outside the scope
Grants	£18,000	outside the scope
Christmas cards	£12,000	standard-rated
Publications	£10,000	zero-rated
Advertising in magazine	£8,000	standard-rated
Bank interest	£4,500	outside the scope
Total income	**£126,500**	

Step 2 *Which of these supplies are taxable?*

Zero-rated and standard-rated items are taxable:

Shop selling donated goods	£24,000	zero-rated
Christmas cards	£12,000	standard-rated
Publications	£10,000	zero-rated
Advertising in magazine	£8,000	standard-rated
Total taxable supplies	**£54,000**	

Step 3 *Does the total of taxable supplies go over the VAT threshold?*

Yes, the total taxable supplies in this example for 2000/01 exceed the registration threshold of £52,000. The charity should register for VAT.

It can be seen from this example that the difference between VAT categories is important. Many misunderstandings arise when zero-rated is taken to mean the same as exempt. These two categories are quite different. An organisation with income of £52,000 (2000/01) from exempt sources will not register; one with income of £52,000 from zero-rated sources should register.

3. Activities of charities

This chapter looks at the various forms of income charities may receive for their direct charitable activities and explains how to establish their VAT category. This includes grants and contracts, as well as education and health and some other activities undertaken by charities. Fundraising income is examined in more detail in the next chapter, but there is some overlap and you may need to refer to it to find a particular type of income as appropriate.

Firstly an overview of the categories of supplies for VAT purposes:

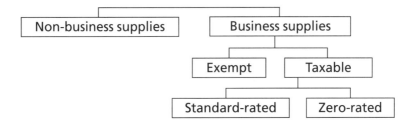

Non-business supplies are outside the scope of VAT, so VAT is not charged on this type of income, nor can VAT on related purchases be recovered. You cannot register for VAT if you only have non-business income.

Business supplies are either exempt or taxable.

▼ Exempt supplies are defined by law and will include many activities by charities, for example education. No VAT can be recovered in general in relation to exempt supplies and you cannot register for VAT if you only make exempt supplies or non-business and exempt supplies.

▼ Taxable supplies bear VAT at either standard, lower or zero rates of VAT, and the VAT has to be added to the price charged to customers. You have to register and charge VAT on these supplies once you go over the VAT registration threshold (*see chapter 2 When do you have to register for VAT?, p12*). You can recover all the associated VAT on purchases.

BUSINESS OR NON-BUSINESS?

Whether VAT is payable or not usually depends on the nature of the supply, not on the status of the supplier.

Charities must take care as a business activity for VAT purposes is not necessarily just profit-making trading. Many of the activities undertaken by a charity will be within the scope of VAT as a business activity. Note, however, that not all business activity is subject to VAT at the standard rate, but may be zero-rated or exempt. 'Business' has a wide meaning for VAT purposes, so it is better to start from the premise that an activity is likely to be business, but then look to see whether the activity does fit in with any of the conditions for non-business activity. If it does fit a definition of a non-business activity, then it can be seen as 'outside the scope' of VAT.

NON-BUSINESS ACTIVITIES

Non-business activities are the more 'traditional' areas of charity income, such as donations, legacies, grants, public collections. It will also include activities where services are provided free to users, or if they do pay, it is well below cost. It may be useful to refer directly to VAT Notice 701/1 'Charities'.

The following are specifically defined as falling outside the scope of VAT as non-business activities:

▼ voluntary services performed free of charge in accordance with the objects of the charity, e.g. rescue at sea, first aid, religious ceremonies. Where a token offering is given, then this is treated as a donation. This is because the service would be performed whether or not the offering were made;

▼ free services such as education provided in state schools where no charge is made;

▼ goods that are given away for free, except when exported, in which case they are zero-rated;

▼ supplies made below cost for the relief of distress, known as welfare services. This includes supplies to persons over 65, physically or mentally handicapped persons, the chronically sick and the poor. 'Below cost' means that a subsidy of at least 15% must be provided towards the cost of the service from the charity's own funds. Grants and donations fundraised for the purpose of subsidising the service will be included in the definition of the charity's own funds (*see also Exempt welfare services in the section on Exempt activities by charities, p26*);

▼ voluntary organisations distributing meals on wheels on behalf of the local authority where the voluntary organisation is acting as the local authority's agent, as the service is then part of the local authority's non-business activity;

▼ donations freely given with the timing, amount and frequency at the discretion of the donor. Stickers and other lapel badges or emblems given in recognition of donations are not considered a sale in this context as their value is insignificant and therefore such donations are fully outside the scope of VAT. These should be restricted to small items designed to be worn on clothing and of a minimal value. Items given in recognition of an anticipated donation of £1 or less fall within these criteria, although the cost of the item should be considerably less than £1. More substantial lapel badges offered for sale to the public where the sale price is specified will be standard-rated business activity;

▼ legacies because they are considered to be donations, even if there is condition attached to the bequest or it has to be applied to a specific activity;

▼ grants which are freely given. They should not be a purchase of services, although the grantor may attach conditions or specify the purpose for which the grant should be used;

▼ investment income such as dividends and interest earned on deposits by charities since a ruling in a case in 1992 (NSPCC, *see Summaries of useful VAT cases*) that investment management and share dealing do not constitute a business activity, since it was not the charity's main purpose;

▼ secondment of staff from one charity or not-profit-making entity to another on the basis of actual salary reimbursement, providing the member of staff is engaged only in the non-business activities of both the lending and borrowing charity;

▼ work placement schemes where a trainee is given work experience by a business. If the business makes payments to the trainees, these would normally be wages and outside the scope of VAT. If the college placing the trainee charges the business a fee, then this would be standard-rated;

▼ membership subscriptions may amount to donations if the members receive few if any benefits. Charities that have a membership scheme that amounts to a means for gaining supporters and raising funds may find that the scheme falls into the category of non-business. Membership income can be complex, however, and is examined in more detail below.

GRANT OR CONTRACT?

There have been particular difficulties with establishing the VAT category applicable to a range of funding agreements which have grown up between government bodies and voluntary organisations. Each case will be looked at on its merits, but it is also possible that different interpretations will be encountered for very similar funding agreements. There have been a number of important VAT cases in recent years that may help us with the underlying principles in operation in this area. A funding agreement will be subject to VAT in the following situations.

▼ There should be a direct link between a particular payment and a particular service.

▼ There must be a legal relationship between the parties involved.

▼ There should be consideration for the service.

There have been two cases where the voluntary organisation wished the funding to be treated as taxable, but this was challenged by Customs & Excise and the voluntary organisation lost. In Bowthorpe Community Trust (*see Summaries of useful VAT cases*), the local authority provided some funding for the training of disabled people and also referred disabled people to the centre. However, it was held that the training service was being provided to the trainees not to the local authority. In Wolverhampton Citizens Advice Bureau (CAB), (*see Summaries of useful VAT cases*) there was a service level agreement with the local authority, so the intention to create a legal binding agreement and a taxable supply for VAT purposes was in evidence in the agreement. Nonetheless, it was held that the CAB was providing a free service to the public and was not providing a service to the local authority.

It is crucial therefore to deal with the question: 'Does the funding body directly receive a benefit from the service provided?' A contract will be a business activity if the public authority is purchasing a service from the voluntary organisation. A grant will not be a business transaction if it provides a subsidy for a service provided to others. Note that the underlying nature of the arrangement is key to getting the right VAT treatment, rather than the documentation or what the arrangement is called.

Another argument put forward against contracts being a business activity is based on an old case, the Apple and Pear Development Council (*see Summaries of useful VAT cases*). Here the argument was put that the council was under a statutory duty to provide the service anyway, so the fees it charged to growers for the services supplied were not consideration for the service.

On the other side of this, there has been a ruling that Legal Aid Board funding is standard-rated where this is part of the legal franchise arrangements, which have been extended to some voluntary organisations providing advice. Although these are similar to grants in the hands of the receiving voluntary organisation, the payments are part of a scheme which sets out to purchase advice services for the public.

This area is still very uncertain, but we have to learn from the cases and rulings we have.

▼ There has to be a *quid pro quo* – an exchange of consideration for a service supplied to the person paying for the service – for a transaction to be categorised as a business transaction for VAT purposes.

▼ A grant subsidy for a service supplied to others is not converted into a purchase of services simply by creating a new legal relationship. If the voluntary organisation would provide the service to that client group anyway, then it is likely that the funding will be a subsidy for a non-business activity.

▼ A voluntary organisation providing services to a public authority will be making a business supply where the public authority is deriving benefit from the supply.

An example of a business contract would be the provision of advice to the tenants of a housing association by an advice charity. This is work that the staff of the housing association would otherwise have undertaken, and a decision has been made to contract out the service.

However, the circumstances of each situation will affect exactly how it should be treated. If in doubt, seek a ruling from your local VAT office.

MEMBERSHIP SUBSCRIPTIONS

Subscriptions and membership can take many forms, so it important to look at what the subscriber receives for their subscription.

▼ Subscriptions to trade unions, professional bodies, learned societies and other not-for-profit organisations in the public domain whose objects are of a political, religious, patriotic, philosophical or philanthropic nature are exempt, providing the benefits members receive are minimal and refer to the objects of the organisation (*see further details under the section on Exempt activities, p26*).

▼ Where nothing is received in return for the subscription then this is substantially a donation and is outside the scope of VAT. This is still the case where minimal benefits are given, such as an annual report and the right to vote at the AGM. This would apply in situations where charities are basically using the subscription as a means of attracting supporters.

▼ Where more substantial benefits are given in return for the subscription, then the whole subscription will be standard-rated, unless another exemption applies or an apportionment (*see box, p26*) is agreed with the VAT office.

▼ Membership of sports clubs and centres will usually be exempt (*see Sport under the section on Exempt activities, p33*).

▼ Membership of arts organisations may be exempt if the subscription entitles the member to admission to a museum, gallery, art exhibition, zoo or performance and the organisation qualifies as an eligible body (*see Cultural services under the section on Exempt activities, p35*).

Values need to be attributed to the various membership benefits by reference to cost or the price non-members pay. Then the VAT category applicable to the goods and services provided as membership benefits determines the VAT rate to apply. This must be agreed with the local VAT office in advance.

> ### Example: Membership subscriptions and apportionment
>
> Membership benefits amount to a free magazine four times a year (normal cost £2.50 to non-members) and a discount on tickets for performances worth approximately £2 per ticket. The overall discounts given last year per the accounting records totalled £24,000. Since there are 3,000 members, this is the equivalent of each member benefiting from discounts of £8 each in a year. The membership subscription is £35 per year. The apportionment could be calculated as follows:
>
> | | | |
> |---|---|---|
> | Magazine | £10 | Zero-rated benefit |
> | Discount on tickets | £ 8 | Standard-rated benefit |
> | Balance = Donation | £17 | Outside the scope |
>
> When apportioning subscriptions, only benefits provided to members in return for the subscription should be taken into account. Benefits that are available to non-members and members alike do not come into the apportionment, likewise items that are free to both members and non-members. The apportionment will not be agreed if the amount of zero-rated or exempt supplies is trivial compared to the benefits provided as a whole.
>
> Life subscriptions will have to be apportioned on a basis that is reasonable. A proposal for the basis should be sent to the VAT office for agreement.
>
> Similarly, different rates of membership will have to be reflected in the apportionment agreed.
>
> Overseas subscriptions will normally follow the same rules and VAT should be charged on the same basis as UK subscriptions.
>
> Remember, any apportionment should be agreed with Customs & Excise *before* it is used as a basis to recover VAT.

EXEMPT ACTIVITIES

There are certain business activities which are exempt from VAT in all situations; there are also certain activities which are exempt when undertaken by a charity. If the activities are exempt, then no VAT should be charged, nor may VAT on related purchases be recovered, unless these activities are minimal (*see chapter 5 on Recovering VAT, p49*). If the organisation mainly undertakes exempt activities, then it will not be able to register for VAT. Similarly, registration will not be available if a combination of non-business and exempt activities are undertaken.

The main exemptions are listed in Schedule 9 to the VAT Act 1994, as updated and amended by case law. The groups to Schedule 9 are listed below:

1 Land

2 Insurance

3 Postal services

4 Betting, gaming and lotteries

5 Finance

6 Education

7 Health and welfare

8 Burial and cremation

9 Subscriptions to trade unions, professional and other public interest bodies

10 Sport, sports competitions and physical education

11 Works of art, etc.

12 Fundraising events by charities and other qualifying bodies

13 Cultural services, etc.

14 Supplies of goods where input tax cannot be recovered

15 Investment gold.

In this section we will look at the following in more detail:

▼ education;
▼ health and welfare;
▼ subscriptions to trade unions, professional and other public interest bodies;
▼ sport, sports competitions and physical education;
▼ cultural services, etc.

Education

Whilst education has a broad meaning for the purposes of charitable status, this is not the case for VAT. Education is not actually defined in the law, but regarded by Customs & Excise as meaning:

a course, class or lesson of instruction or study in any subject, whether or not normally taught in schools, colleges or universities and regardless of where and when it takes place. Education includes lectures, educational seminars, conferences and symposia, together with holiday, sporting and recreational courses. It also includes distance teaching and associated materials, if the student is subject to assessment by the teaching institution.

The provision of education by an *eligible body* is exempt from VAT, as provided for in the VAT Act 1994, Schedule 9 Group 6.

An eligible body is:

▼ a recognised school;

▼ a UK college or university;

▼ further education institutions (including the Workers' Educational Association and any other bodies that have been designated as such under various education acts);

▼ government departments, local authorities, health authorities and executive agencies of government;

▼ organisations providing teaching of English as a foreign language (but the exemption only applies to the tuition in EFL);

▼ a not-for-profit body, providing its constitution prohibits the distribution of profits and it does not in fact distribute any profits. In addition, any profits made from exempt educational supplies including research and vocational training must be applied to the continuance or improvement of those activities.

Clearly most charities would qualify as eligible bodies and education and training services they provide will therefore qualify for exemption, providing they use any profit to further the educational activities.

Note that if you do not want the activity to be exempt, then training by a for-profit body is standard-rated, as is training by a charity when the profits are applied to another activity.

Charities will operate a number of different activities falling within the education exemption, which are clarified below. Note that the overall condition that the supply must be made by an eligible body applies in all cases.

Vocational training

Vocational training means training, re-training or the provision of work experience for any trade, profession or employment; or for any voluntary work of a charitable nature (including education, health, safety or welfare). The net is cast widely and vocational training will apply to courses, conferences, lectures, workshops and seminars. The training can be for those already in work, where the intention is to improve their knowledge in order to improve their performance in work, or to prepare people for future work. So, for example, a conference organised by a charity for employees and voluntary workers (including trustees) to provide information and discuss current topics will be vocational training and therefore exempt.

It does not include consultancy designed to improve the efficiency or smooth-running of the whole organisation, which should be standard-rated. Individual counselling is also excluded from this category, although it may be exempt if it is part of a training package.

Contracts with training and enterprise councils (TECs) and successor bodies

There are various schemes for vocational training that are government sponsored, and whilst the actual schemes have changed over the years, they have always been specifically exempt from VAT. So contracts with TECs will be exempt for VAT purposes, as are training courses funded by the European Social Fund (ESF) and the education funding councils in the UK. The management and administration of the contract is exempt if this is included in the overall supply, but would be standard-rated if the contract allowed for a separate supply of management services. Future bodies established with similar purposes, such as the Learning and Skills Councils, will probably continue the arrangement.

New Deal

The various elements of the New Deal can be identified as either:

▼ vocational training (and therefore exempt);

▼ subsidy of wages (and therefore outside the scope);

▼ one-to-one counselling or awareness training (usually a standard-rated supply to the Employment Service).

Detailed guidance on the VAT liability of various elements of the New Deal is available from Customs & Excise in their VAT Information Sheet 3/99 (also on their website).

Youth clubs

Subscriptions to youth clubs are exempt, as is any other payment by members for the ordinary activities of the youth club. A youth club is a club established to promote the social, physical, educational or spiritual development of its members which is run by a charity or other not-for-profit organisation fulfilling the criteria of an eligible body. The members of the club should be mainly under 21, which means that at least 51% of the members should be 20 or less. Youth clubs should be separately constituted and the youth sections of sports clubs and the like are not regarded as youth clubs. Other activities organised by the youth club will not necessarily be exempt, such as holidays and sales of food and drink.

Research

Without a statutory definition, we rely on the interpretation given in VAT Notices. Thus research is 'original investigation undertaken in order to gain knowledge and understanding'.

The intention at the beginning of a project determines whether a supply qualifies as research, and the intention should be to advance knowledge and understanding. Merely confirming existing knowledge is not research, nor is consultancy, market research, writing software or testing components. The fact that the research may have a commercial application does not in itself exclude it from the exemption. However, the supply of research services to a commercial body is standard-rated, whereas supplies between eligible bodies are exempt (even if the recipient is not involved in the field of education).

Examination fees

Examination services provided by eligible bodies to individuals or other eligible bodies are exempt. This includes assessment and setting training standards.

Ancillary supplies

Schools and other bodies often sell additional goods and services to pupils and trainees. Some of these will not fall within the exemption, but some are closely related to the main supply of education and are exempt. Examples of closely related supplies are accommodation, catering, transport and school trips. They have to be for the direct use of the student and necessary for the delivery of education to that student. Sales from vending machines, shops, bars, uniform sales and other separately charged services will not be closely related to the supply of education, and VAT will apply as normal. To qualify for the exemption, the goods or services should be for the direct use of the pupil or student, or the exemption can apply where the school (or other eligible body) is buying in related services from another eligible body.

Health and welfare

There is a general exemption for health and medical services provided by registered medical practitioners. The profession has to be statutorily registered, so practitioners such as acupuncturists and reflexologists are excluded, whereas osteopaths are included in the exemption. So services from opticians, nurses and dentists are all exempt. Note that the exemption does not extend to all supplies, so for example spectacles are standard-rated, unless supplied in hospital or as low-vision aids for the severely visually impaired.

There are a number of activities provided by charities which are exempt under the health and welfare group. Mostly these are exempt whether provided by a charity or not, except for certain welfare services as explained below.

Exempt welfare services

The exemption covers provision of welfare services 'otherwise than for a profit'. This means services directly connected with:

▼ the provision of care, treatment or instruction designed to promote the physical or mental welfare of elderly, sick, distressed or disabled persons;

▼ the protection of children and young persons; or

▼ the provision of spiritual welfare by a religious institution as part of a course of instruction or a retreat.

'Otherwise than for a profit' means that even if a surplus is made, it is applied solely to the furtherance of the activity which generated the surplus. However, note the ruling in the Bell Concord case (*see Summaries of useful VAT cases*), which recognised that the main activity of the charity was the activity generating the profit.

'Care' was the subject of the case Watford Help in the Home(*see Summaries of useful VAT cases*). Previously narrowly defined by Customs & Excise as relating only to personal care services such as bathing, dressing wounds, toiletting and help with dressing, the Watford Help in the Home case showed that care could mean domestic help services such as cleaning, cooking and shopping. Domestic help is an exempt welfare service when supplied to 'people for whom there is either current or imminent substantial risk to the health and welfare of the person and who are unable to provide even basic self care or who have major difficulty in safely carrying out some key daily living tasks'. Consequently, Customs & Excise do expect some form of assessment to take place to confirm that the person is in need of the domestic help.

Registered homes

The exemption applies to the provision of care, including accommodation and catering, in nursing homes and residential care homes registered under the Registered Homes Act 1984 (or equivalent in Scotland). This covers homes for the elderly, people with past or present dependency on drugs or alcohol and people with past or present mental disorder.

Probation and bail hostels

Probation and bail hostels (and their equivalent in Scotland) are exempt where the services are provided under the Powers of Criminal Courts Act 1973.

Supervised care

Care by unqualified staff will be exempt if the staff are properly supervised by a qualified person. The supervision has to be direct, on a one-to-one basis and not through an intermediary. The supervisor does not have to be on the same premises the whole time, but should be readily available for the whole of the time the unqualified staff are working. The supervisor should see the client at the outset of treatment or care and at appropriate intervals subsequently. The work of the unqualified staff should require supervision and be of a medical or caring nature. You could not convert a cleaning service into an exempt nursing service by employing a supervisor who happened to be a qualified nurse. There are detailed guidelines agreed between Customs & Excise and representative bodies, which should be consulted if you wish to use this exemption.

Nurseries

Nurseries and playgroups providing care to children and which are registered under the Children Act 1989 are exempt.

Hospital trolleys

Where charities provide services to patients in hospitals or registered care homes that are part of the accommodation, catering, medical or nursing services, then these will be exempt. Included are refreshments such as tea and coffee. Supplies to visitors and supplies of alcohol are excluded from the exemption.

Subscriptions to trade unions, professional and other public interest bodies

Since 1 December 1999 subscriptions to trade unions and other bodies in the public domain are exempt, whereas they were previously treated by Customs & Excise as non-business. The organisations that are affected are non-profit making organisations whose aims are in the public domain and are of a political, religious, patriotic, philosophical, philanthropic or civic nature. Not all of these will be charities, obviously, but some of the bodies whose membership subscriptions are covered by the exemption include:

▼ trade unions;
▼ professional bodies;
▼ trade associations;
▼ learned societies;
▼ political parties;
▼ think tanks and pressure groups.

In order for the exemption to apply, the only benefits to members should:

- ▼ relate to the aims of the organisation; and
- ▼ be provided in return for the subscription; and
- ▼ not include a right of admission to premises or events for which non-members have to pay.

In other words, membership benefits have to be minimal for the exemption to apply. If greater benefits are given in return for a subscription, then the subscription will be treated as taxable unless an apportionment is agreed with the VAT office in advance where there are further benefits that should be exempt or zero-rated.

Where the organisation had already obtained agreement from the VAT office on the apportionment of membership subscriptions, for example agreeing that a proportion of the subscription related to zero-rated publications, then the agreement still stands.

Where members receive no benefits, then subscriptions may still be treated as donations and therefore non-business.

Sport, sports competitions and physical education

Sports or physical recreation is not defined in the legislation but is taken to include any activity that is recognised as a sporting activity by the Sports Council. For certain exemptions to apply the sport must involve some physical exertion. In addition, exemption will only apply in some circumstances where an *eligible* body is involved. Note that the rules were changed for exempting sporting activity on 1 January 2000, and these are the basis of this section.

An eligible body is a not-for-profit organisation:

- ▼ with a prohibition in its constitution on the distribution of profits, other than transfer to another not-for-profit organisation on winding up;

- ▼ spending any surplus it does generate from the exempt sporting activity to the maintenance and improvement of facilities, or on the objects of the organisation;

- ▼ which is not subject to 'commercial influence'. This term refers to any transactions with the committee members, such as purchasing services or renting premises from them or their companies. Payments to committee members and performance related bonuses would also amount to commercial influence. Specifically management and administration services and property transactions supplied by a committee member would create commercial influence. A supply of other goods and services under normal terms should not create commercial influence, but it would be advisable to agree this with your VAT office. Transactions with other charities and local authorities will not be caught under the definition of commercial influence, even if representatives from those bodies are on the management committee. This is a complex area of anti-avoidance legislation and so if you think you may be caught by it, check the guidance issued by Customs & Excise on this point (*see Specific guidance relevant to charities under Further information, p122*). For most charities providing sporting facilities, it is unlikely that there will be problems and you should be able to treat charges as exempt.

An eligible body cannot be a public body such as a local authority or government body.

The sections below explain what the exemption covers.

▼ Services closely linked with and essential to sport or physical recreation supplied to individuals taking part in the activity provided by an eligible body are exempt. The term 'individuals' includes families, but spectators are excluded as they are not taking part.

▼ Entry fees and admission fees to sporting facilities run by an eligible body such as swimming pools and sports centres are exempt.

▼ Ancillary services such as use of changing rooms, showers and playing equipment, as well as umpiring services, coaching, training and physical education are exempt.

▼ Membership subscriptions and joining fees for participating in sporting activities are exempt. Access to the club bar is a benefit, but seen as integral to the membership and therefore it can be included in the exemption. However, if a significant element of the membership subscription is related to other benefits, then it may be necessary to apportion the subscription and to standard-rate certain elements. If you wish to zero-rate elements that relate to printed matter, then it will be necessary to review the whole subscription for apportionment, including the social element.

▼ Exemption does not extend to catering, accommodation or transport services, nor to admission charges for spectators.

▼ Subscriptions to sports governing bodies are exempt insofar as they can be attributed to 'services closely linked and essential to sport' supplied to individuals or sports clubs. Affiliation fees are frequently calculated on the basis of a head count of the members in the club, so this would still qualify for the exemption. Additional services provided, such as priority booking for international matches and similar benefits, are not exempt and should be standard-rated.

Sports competitions

Entry fees to competitions in sport or physical recreation organised by anyone are exempt, providing the entry fee is entirely used to provide the prizes. In addition, eligible bodies established for the purposes of sport or physical recreation can exempt the entry fees to competitions. The sports that can be included are extended in this case to include dancing, darts and pigeon racing. Note that local authorities are not within this definition as they are not established for the purposes of sport or physical recreation.

Renting out sports facilities

Short-term lets are standard-rated, but letting out facilities for more than 24 hours or a series of lettings to the same person may be exempt. This will apply to letting out a village hall for badminton as well as letting out facilities in a purpose built sports centre. A series of ten or more lettings to a school, club or association will be exempt where the same activity takes place and the activity is regular, for example weekly or fortnightly. The exemption can also apply if sports facilities are let out for non-sporting purposes on a regular basis, for example if a sports hall is let out for a meeting. The letting fees are covered by the exemption. Sports facilities can include dance studios and any premises that have been designed or equipped specifically for a sporting or physical education purpose. Ancillary services can be included in the exemption, but this does not extend to the provision of optional extras of either equipment or staff, which should therefore be standard-rated. (*See VAT Notice 742/1 'Letting of facilities for sport and physical recreation'.*)

Cultural services

This exemption was introduced in 1996 as a result of a case in Europe concerning the Italian government. The British government is obliged to implement the EC Sixth Directive in all matters, and the Italian case highlighted that governments had not correctly implemented this point. Article 13A(1)(n) of the Sixth Directive provides for the exemption from VAT of certain 'cultural services' provided by public bodies and *eligible* bodies.

The cultural services that are covered are:

▼ admission charges to museums, galleries, art exhibitions, zoos;

▼ admission charges for theatrical, musical or choreographic performance of a cultural nature.

The normal meaning of the words 'museum, gallery, art exhibition or zoo' should be used to interpret the application of the law in this area, but Customs & Excise will also take into account the nature of the exhibits and whether the organisation is, for example, a member of a representative body. A 'performance' can be any form of stage play, opera, musical comedy, classical music, jazz, ballet or dance to fall within the meaning of the term 'cultural'. (*See VAT Notice 701/47 'Culture' for further details.*)

An eligible body:

▼ is not a public body;

▼ is prohibited under its constitution from distributing a profit and does not in practice distribute profits;

▼ applies any profits from the exempt admission fees to furthering the activities covered by the exemption or improving the relevant facilities;

▼ is managed and administered on a voluntary basis by people who have no direct or indirect financial interest in its activities. This particular condition has been tested in two VAT tribunal cases. In the Glastonbury Abbey case (*see Summaries of useful VAT cases*) Customs & Excise lost and it was stated that the UK law had omitted a key word, 'essentially', in the Sixth Directive. Thus the UK law should read 'managed and administered on an essentially voluntary basis'. The Zoological Society of London (*see Summaries of useful VAT cases*) has also challenged Customs & Excise on their interpretation of this term, arguing that a voluntary board of trustees was responsible for the management and administration of the charity. Whilst some executive functions were delegated to a professional management team, the responsibility was not delegated. The court has referred the proper interpretation of the term to the European court, so it maybe some time before this matter is finally decided. In the meantime, it is possible for small organisations to be eligible under this criterion as the Glastonbury case showed. The employment of staff undertaking activities relevant to the operation of the service will not prevent an organisation exempting entry fees under this section, but the staff should not be involved in the management or administration of the organisation. Larger museums and galleries are generally taken to have paid professional management and administration and therefore charge VAT on their admission fees.

Note that the exemption is also available to public bodies, such as local authorities, but they must ensure that no distortion of competition will be caused by the exemption of admission fees to their premises. They have to notify relevant commercial undertakings in their area to give them an opportunity to object, and if objections are received they have to ask the VAT office for a ruling.

ZERO-RATED SUPPLIES

Some activities undertaken by charities will be zero-rated. These are part of the taxable supplies of an organisation and therefore they will count towards the threshold for registration, and VAT on purchases relating to these activities will be fully recoverable.

Activities falling within the scope of VAT but zero-rated are listed in Schedule 8 to the VAT Act 1994. The groups are:

1 Food

2 Sewerage services and water

3 Books, etc.

4 Talking books for the blind and handicapped and wireless sets for the blind

5 Construction of buildings, etc.

ACTIVITIES OF CHARITIES

6   Protected buildings

7   International services

8   Transport

9   Caravans and houseboats

10 Gold

11 Bank notes

12 Drugs, medicines, aids for the handicapped, etc.

13 Imports, exports, etc.

14 [deleted from the schedule]

15 Charities, etc.

16 Clothing and footwear.

The main importance of the zero-rated items for charities is that these are goods or services that charities buy and so being able to buy them without VAT represents a significant saving. This aspect of VAT is covered in chapter 6 (*see p61*).

The main focus of this section is to look at the common activities of charities other than fundraising and establish the VAT status of those activities. Zero-rated activities of charities may include:

▼ sale of books, newsletters and printed matter. Zero-rating does not extend to cassettes, videotapes, CD-ROMs nor information provided electronically over the internet. Chapter 6 provides more detail on exactly what form the printed item needs to take to qualify for zero-rating, and this will apply to sales by the charity as well as purchases;

▼ membership subscriptions where the principal supply provided under the membership scheme is printed matter, such as magazines, newsletters, reports. In this case it will be necessary to get clearance from Customs & Excise in advance, providing details of the benefits given to members and the subscriptions they pay;

▼ sale of donated goods (*see chapter 4, p45, for full details*);

▼ the export of goods outside the EC. This applies to any goods exported by a charity to a country outside the EC, even when the activity would normally fall outside the scope of VAT as a non-business activity. For example, charities giving away goods overseas as part of a relief effort will be able to treat this activity as zero-rated export, and therefore recover VAT on the purchase of the goods;

▼ transport services in vehicles designed to carry twelve or more passengers. If the vehicle has been adapted to carry a wheelchair so that the carrying capacity has been reduced, then the services will still be zero-rated.

37

A PRACTICAL GUIDE TO VAT

STANDARD-RATED ACTIVITIES

Many other activities of charities will fall within the category of standard-rated. It is wise to assume that if you cannot find a specific category to treat an activity as non-business, exempt or zero-rated, then it should be standard-rated. Examples of many fundraising activities that are standard-rated are covered in chapter 4 (*see p39*). Some of the activities undertaken by charities in fulfilling their charitable activities that may be standard-rated are:

▼ sales of audio cassettes, videos, CD-ROMs;

▼ sales of advertising space;

▼ advice and consultancy services;

▼ admission fees where the cultural exemption does not apply;

▼ catering in cafes, bars, etc.;

▼ royalties;

▼ charges for postage and packing;

▼ photocopying charged out to others;

▼ charges for services to trading subsidiaries or other members of the group, unless group registration is in operation (*see chapter 9 Planning for VAT, p97*).

4 ▾ Fundraising

This chapter looks at the VAT categories that apply to the activities of charities which are aimed specifically at raising funds for the work of the charity. Charities receive funding in a number of ways, and some of the funding methods may have been covered in the previous chapter. This chapter covers many forms of fundraising, such as sponsorship, events and selling goods.

The VAT status of an activity will depend on how it is organised. For example, collecting donations will be outside the scope of VAT and does not count as a business activity. However, charities may use several methods to obtain donations, alongside selling goods and inviting members of the public to participate in events. Hence the VAT position may be fairly complex for a fundraising activity. It is important that the VAT status is established at the outset. It may be possible to arrange the transactions so that the VAT treatment is beneficial to the charity.

The specific areas of fundraising activity examined in more detail below are:

- ▾ collecting donations;
- ▾ sponsorship;
- ▾ cause-related marketing;
- ▾ corporate events;
- ▾ affinity credit cards;
- ▾ fundraising events;
- ▾ challenge events;
- ▾ lotteries;
- ▾ bingo;

- ▾ shops;
- ▾ sale of donated goods;
- ▾ charity auctions;
- ▾ Christmas cards;
- ▾ merchandising;
- ▾ services to other charities;
- ▾ selling advertising space;
- ▾ gifts in kind from companies and barter arrangements.

For raising income from renting out premises, see chapter 8 Property.

Fundraising is constantly changing and new ideas come forward all the time. It is therefore important to grasp the underlying principles to use in all fundraising situations even if the particular situation is not covered here.

▾ VAT only applies to business transactions, so donations and grants are outside the scope of VAT. So are other donated goods and services, providing they are given without any expectation of a benefit in return.

▼ In general, the sale of goods or services will be subject to VAT, unless covered by a specific zero-rating or exemption. A considerable amount of charitable activity is exempt (*see chapter 3 Activities of charities*) and certain fundraising activities will be exempt or zero-rated. However, the closer you get to straightforward commercial arrangements, the more likely it is that you should be charging VAT.

▼ Underlying all VAT law is a consideration that the tax rules should not distort competition. If a charity has an unfair advantage because of its charitable status yet is competing with commercial traders, then it is likely that the charity is on the edge of what is permitted by law and there may be a challenge to the treatment by Customs & Excise.

▼ The VAT treatment needs to be sorted out *before* you start the activity, as it will be too late afterwards to change the wording on the leaflet, advertisement or other documentation.

COLLECTING DONATIONS

Charities may use several methods for collecting donations, including shaking tins, regular envelope collections in churches, telephone fundraising, direct mail, house-to-house collections and many more. The basic principle here is that money freely given to a charity with no expectation of goods or services in return is outside the scope of VAT as it is not a business activity. If the charity provides any service then it is not freely given and you need to consider whether VAT should apply.

The charity cannot reclaim VAT on purchases directly relating to collecting donations, but it can reduce its VAT burden by purchasing goods at zero rates of VAT. Collecting tins, lapel badges and fundraising advertisements and literature will qualify for zero-rating, although direct mail letters may not qualify (since 1 April 2000). *See chapter 6 Saving VAT, p61, for more details of zero-rating on purchases.*

SPONSORSHIP

Corporate donations may in fact be sponsorship and great care is needed. The same principle described above applies: you need to check to see the company is not receiving a service in return for its 'donation'. It is often the case that the company is receiving advertising or promotional services in return for its funding. If the company's logo is being reproduced on publications, leaflets, posters or even a vehicle, then this is likely to be interpreted as a promotional service by Customs & Excise. This service is standard-rated for VAT. A simple acknowledgement will not create a taxable supply, so mentioning the company's name in the annual report or in small print on the back of a publication will not change a donation into a promotional service. Generally it is the use of the company's logo, together with a consideration of the size and prominence of its position that will create a sale of advertising rather than a donation.

Frequently the amount being given by the company is in excess of the value of the service being provided. It is possible to split the amount into an element which is a payment for promotional services, which should be invoiced and VAT applied if you are registered for VAT, and a donation. However, you need to make this explicit from the outset and document appropriately. It is unlikely that you could obtain a retrospective agreement from Customs & Excise to a split. It would be normal to expect VAT on the full amount paid, as demonstrated by the Tron Theatre case (*see Summaries of useful VAT cases*).

However, note that sponsorship income for a fundraising event is exempt, because all supplies of the event are exempt (*see section on Fundraising events, p42*).

Sponsorship of the type where an individual undertakes an activity and friends and relatives support the effort by giving an amount to the nominated charity will be outside the scope of VAT. This is effectively donated income and no service is being provided in return for the monies given.

CAUSE-RELATED MARKETING

Cause-related marketing is really sponsorship in reverse: companies value charity brands and may wish to pay the charity a fee (usually under a licence agreement for the right to use your charity name and logo for a certain period of time). It is a commercial arrangement and is standard-rated for VAT. It may be structured as a royalty; this is still standard-rated for VAT.

The charity may receive donations in addition to the licence fee. The donations will be outside the scope of VAT, but the arrangement must make it clear that the donations are quite separate. These arrangements should be documented in an agreement, as the company is a commercial participator under the Fundraising Regulations of the Charities Act 1993. In such an agreement it is necessary to set out clearly what is a fee and what is a donation.

CORPORATE EVENTS

Companies may organise an event in order to raise funds for charity, or a charity may organise an event for a company. These are often particular days at major sporting occasions such as horse racing.

If the company organises an event and states that it intends to donate money raised to a charity, then the charity is not responsible for the financial arrangements. The charity merely receives a donation after the event, which is outside the scope of VAT.

If the charity organises the event it is likely to be a fundraising event and therefore exempt. However, you do need to fulfil the criteria of fundraising events. So, for example, it should be clear that the event is for the purpose of raising funds for your charity. Corporate events that are sold as a team-building exercise may fall outside the scope of the fundraising event definition and may be standard-rated supplies.

AFFINITY CREDIT CARDS

These are credit cards carrying a charity name and logo. The credit card company has the use of the charity's mailing list and some assistance in recruiting the charity's members and supporters as subscribers to the card. The charity usually receives a fixed payment on first use of the card and an agreed percentage of all retail spending thereafter. There should be a proper written agreement which allows for the use of the charity's name and logo and mailing list. In practice, there are usually two agreements. The first of these is between the credit card company and the charity's trading subsidiary for the assistance in recruiting members, which is a standard-rated supply. The second agreement is between the charity and credit card company allowing use of the logo.

Customs & Excise have agreed that it is appropriate to regard a proportion of the initial payment to the charity, usually 20%, as a fee for use of the charity name and mailing list. All the rest is treated as a donation (*see VAT Notice 701/1/95*).

FUNDRAISING EVENTS

Changes to the VAT and tax exemptions for fundraising events were made from 1 April 2000.

Fundraising events no longer have to be one-off: charities may have 15 events of the same kind in the same location in one financial year. Events may be held by the charity or its trading subsidiary, but the limit of 15 would apply to them jointly.

'Events' can be widely interpreted. An event on the internet will qualify for the exemption, as will participatory events such as golf days. In addition, charges made to spectators at events will fall within the exemption. Exempt fundraising events may include gala dinners, premiere nights, dinner dances and any other events organised for a fundraising purpose. If performances run for several nights, the limit is 15 and each performance is treated as a single fundraising event. If the charity exceeds the limit and organises 16 similar events in one location, then the exemption would be lost for all 16. Regular or continuous activities, such as weekly parachute jumps or sales of Christmas cards would be excluded.

Adventure or challenge events such as parachute and bungee jumps will also be included in the exemption as long as any accommodation provided does not exceed two nights and the event does not fall within the Tour Operators' Margin Scheme (*see section on Challenge events, below*).

Events do have to be organised with a clear fundraising purpose, which should be made known to the public. Any events which create a distortion of competition and place a commercial enterprise at a disadvantage will not be exempt fundraising events.

Small-scale events can be ignored, as long as the aggregate gross takings from events of that type in that location do not exceed £1,000 in a week. This means that jumble sales and coffee mornings are not included when counting up the number of events and are exempt from VAT.

All income at the fundraising event will be covered by the exemption, including entry fees, sponsorship, advertising space, sale of brochures and commemorative items, unless they would normally be zero-rated, in which case the zero-rating prevails.

CHALLENGE EVENTS

Challenge events usually involve participants undertaking some activity for which they have raised sponsorship from friends and relatives, for example cycling across a desert or undertaking the Three Peaks Challenge.

Some challenge events will qualify as exempt fundraising events if they do not provide any accommodation or the accommodation is incidental, which means no more than two nights. If the activity is regular, then the charity just has to be careful not to exceed the 15 events limit. For example, a charity raising funds through fun runs will be able to organise a number of these days around the country. However, it cannot hold more than 15 runs in a year in one place if it wishes to stay within the exemption.

However if the charity organises an event which includes the provision of travel and accommodation, then it may come within the Tour Operator's Margin Scheme (TOMS), depending on the way the challenge event is being organised.

TOMS will apply if the charity is buying in travel and accommodation and supplying these on to participants on challenge events. TOMS will not apply if:

▼ participants purchase their travel and accommodation direct from the travel agent/tour operator;

▼ the travel company organises the event and makes a donation to the charity for every place booked.

Frequently the arrangement is that participants have to raise a minimum amount of sponsorship to be eligible to participate, but travel costs can be paid from the sponsorship raised. A 'minimum amount of sponsorship' is effectively the same as specifying an entry fee. If participants are only allowed on the trip if they pay this amount, then this is an entry fee and the charity is providing a service in return. The charity is organising a package event and TOMS applies.

Under TOMS, the sale price of the tour (presumably the minimum sponsorship and any other charges, such as registration fees) is matched against the cost of the tour. The 'margin' or gross profit is the basis for calculating the amount of VAT due to Customs & Excise. No VAT can be recovered on invoices for the cost of the tour. No VAT invoice should be issued to participants.

However, holidays enjoyed outside the EC fall within the zero-rates of VAT. So you may have a situation where the TOMS applies, but the event is taking place outside the EC. In this case there is a zero-rated VATable supply equivalent to the margin of income over costs. No VAT has to be charged, but this does have an effect on the overall VAT position of the charity, usually helping the charity to recover more VAT on costs.

Additional sponsorship raised by individuals will be donations collected by the individual and passed on to the charity. These donations are outside the scope of VAT and are not trading.

Registration fees are often charged in addition to the requirement to raise sponsorship. These are within the scope of VAT, but the VAT treatment will vary. Registration fees may be part of the price charged if the event is within TOMS, or they may be regarded as an exempt entry fee if the event qualifies as a fundraising event. The registration fees could be standard-rated if the challenge event is neither in TOMS nor an exempt fundraising event.

The costs of advertising for participants may well fall within the special relief for charities and therefore be at zero-rate. Note that the advertisement has to be placed by a charity. The relief does not apply to the travel company advertising for participants.

LOTTERIES

The sale of lottery or raffle tickets is exempt from VAT. Whilst there is no statutory definition of a lottery, it has been defined in a case as 'the distribution of prizes by chance where the persons talking part in the operation, or a substantial number of them, make a payment or consideration in return for obtaining their chance of a prize'. Where any merit or skill plays a part in determining the outcome, then it is a competition not a lottery. Competition entry fees are generally standard-rated.

For the organiser, the value of the exempt supply is the net proceeds after deducting the VAT-inclusive cost of goods given as prizes.

Many charities organise fundraising that amounts to a lottery or raffle, because there is a prize distributed on the basis of chance. For example, 'guess the name of the teddy bear' is considered a lottery as it is more chance than skill if you guess the correct name and win the prize.

Note that lotteries are covered by the Lotteries and Amusement Act 1976 and may have to be regulated by the Gaming Board. You need to get a licence to operate a lottery or raffle unless it is a private lottery restricted to the members of a club or a small lottery at an event. Further information should be obtained from the Gaming Board.

If you use the services of a lottery management company, then the charge for the service, however made, is subject to VAT at standard rate.

BINGO

Generally the total amount charged to play bingo is exempt. For the organiser, the value of the exempt supply is the net proceeds after deducting the VAT inclusive cost of goods given as prizes. Generally, charities will be involved in small-scale bingo in clubs or as part of a fundraising activity.

▼ Small-scale cash bingo in clubs will be under the Gaming Act 1968. The club must have at least 25 members, not be temporary in nature and have other activities in addition. The participation charge should be no more than 50p, although there is no limit on the stake money as long as this is all returned to the players as prizes. Only members and their bona fide guests may participate.

▼ Fundraising bingo at a function may be open to the public, but the total participation fee (whether a stake or entrance fee) may not exceed £3. The total value of prizes must not generally exceed £300 per day. The proceeds must be applied to a charitable or not-for-profit purpose.

In both these cases, the amounts paid are exempt. Commercial bingo houses charge an admission fee and sometimes charge a membership fee, both of which are standard-rated. The stake money is, however, exempt.

SHOPS

Donated goods sold in a shop are zero-rated, but bought-in goods are standard-rated, unless they are covered by another zero-rating, such as books.

SALE OF DONATED GOODS

The sale of donated goods is zero-rated, whether the sale is through a shop or not, and the sales may be through a trading subsidiary. The goods may be new or second-hand, but must be donated for the purpose of a sale or hire and should be available for purchase by the general public. So sales through charity shops are zero-rated, as are sales at fundraising events, such as auctions.

Since 1 April 2000, charities or their subsidiaries may also sell donated goods to disabled people and those on means-tested benefits; this did not come within the relief before this date. This will help the schemes whereby recycled furniture is sold at low prices to those in need as now no VAT has to be charged. The new rules also allow the hire or export of the donated goods to be zero-rated.

By concession, Customs & Excise also allows the sale of rags and unwanted donated goods to scrap merchants to be zero-rated.

This is a valuable relief, but there are conditions and anti-avoidance rules.

▼ The relief only applies to goods, not services. In particular it cannot apply to land.

▼ It does not apply to donated raffle prizes

▼ The goods must be donated for the purpose of a sale or hire, not for the charity's own use. The charity may not use them while they are waiting to sell or hire them.

▼ The relief does not apply where goods are donated and used to make other goods for sale (for example, if a donated painting is used to make prints for resale).

▼ Pre-arranged sales will not be eligible for zero-rating. Likewise an arrangement by the donor of the goods with the charity or a purchaser will exclude the sale from the scheme. Thus zero-rating will not apply to schemes where the charity collects used goods such as laser printer cartridges from businesses and then sells them on to one pre-arranged purchaser.

CHARITY AUCTIONS

Charity auctions at a fundraising event will be covered by the overall exemption for all income at the event, unless the goods being sold in the auction are donated, in which case they can be zero-rated. An auction can itself be a fundraising event, although again if the goods for the auction have been donated, then the proceeds from the sale are zero-rated.

CHRISTMAS CARDS

The sale of greeting cards is standard-rated.

MERCHANDISING

Generally, goods sold by a charity to raise funds will be standard-rated, unless covered by a zero-rating. So mugs, tee-shirts and other items will be standard-rated, even if they have the charity's name and logo on them. Goods sold at a fundraising event will be covered by the exemption for the event, unless the goods are zero-rated, such as books or children's tee-shirts.

SERVICES TO OTHER CHARITIES

The sale of services to other charities will normally be standard-rated. An educational charity may exempt the provision of educational services to another charity, such as letting out conference facilities. It may also be possible to treat the secondment of staff as outside the scope where one charity is seconding the member of staff to another to work on non-business activities.

SELLING ADVERTISING SPACE

Generally the sale of advertising is standard-rated, with a few exceptions.

▼ Advertising in the programme or brochure for a fundraising event will be seen as part of the income from the event and will therefore be exempt.

▼ Advertising from private individuals in a charity publication can mean that the income is treated as a donation. This will apply if at least 50% of the advertisements are clearly from private individuals where there is no promotion of commercial objectives. Advertisements from businesses are not from private individuals even if there is no specific reference to a particular trade or service. If the 50% rule is broken then standard-rating applies to all the advertisements.

▼ Selling advertising space to another charity will be zero-rated, providing the conditions are met (*see chapter 6 Saving VAT*).

GIFTS IN KIND FROM COMPANIES AND BARTER ARRANGEMENTS

Companies donating goods to a charity are making a zero-rated supply. If the charity sells the donated goods, then this will be zero-rated provided the conditions are met (*see section on Sale of donated goods, p45*). If the goods are used for the charity's own activities then there are no VAT consequences.

If the company provides goods or services in return for advertising or promotion of its name, then this amounts to a barter arrangement and is subject to VAT under the normal rules.

Example: Barter arrangements

A company offers to print the charity's annual report for free. The company does, however, want its logo in a prominent position on the annual report. The charity is providing advertising space to the company in return for the printing of the annual report. There are, in fact, two transactions, which have been netted off. VAT has to be accounted for on the advertising service. The deemed value of this will be the cost to the company of printing the annual report. The charity can either issue an invoice to the company for the VAT amount or treat the value received as inclusive of VAT and remit the appropriate amount to Customs & Excise. The company in this situation has no VAT to remit, as the printing of an annual report is zero-rated.

It may have been simpler to avoid this situation by:

▼ simply acknowledging the donation of the free printing in the text of the annual report in plain type without prominent display of the logo;

▼ alternatively, charging the company a fee for advertising in the annual report. The company could charge for printing the annual report, perhaps offering a discount.

5 ▼ Recovering VAT

This chapter explains the rules for claiming VAT back from Customs & Excise and provides examples for the various different situations charities experience. There is further information on the book-keeping implications of VAT recovery calculations in chapter 10. This chapter also gives some general guidance on improving the recovery rate of charities.

If you are not registered for VAT you cannot recover input VAT. Once registered for VAT, you record all the VAT on purchases of goods and services. The quarterly total is entered onto the VAT return and reduces the amount of VAT to be paid over to Customs & Excise. As a consequence, the real cost of the goods and services you buy excludes the VAT charged.

Conversely, if you are not registered for VAT, you simply record in your books the total price paid for all goods and services including the VAT element. You do not have to complete VAT returns.

Input VAT is defined as the VAT on purchases relating to business activities and this is the VAT that may be recoverable, subject to restrictions where the organisation undertakes exempt activities (*see the section on Partial exemption, p51*). For charities, this means that expenditure relating to non-business activities must be excluded when completing VAT returns. Any organisation or business may not recover input VAT on certain items of expenditure:

▼ where there is no VAT receipt;

▼ purchase of new cars, unless used exclusively for business;

▼ entertaining;

▼ non-business petrol consumption.

In most commercial organisations and a few charities, the VAT position is relatively simple as all the activities are business activities and all VAT can be recovered. However, for most charities, the mix of activities undertaken by the charity means that they will be able to recover VAT on some activities and not on others.

49

IDENTIFYING THE RECOVERABLE VAT

In order to identify the recoverable element, you have to relate the purchases to the activities for VAT purposes. VAT guidance describes this as 'attributing' input VAT to the appropriate category. This first step looks for input VAT which can be directly attributed to a particular activity.

After this, you will have some input VAT which cannot be directly attributed to one particular area because the purchases are part of the shared costs for the organisation as a whole. This is termed the 'residual' input VAT.

The next step is to apportion the residual VAT to the activities in fair proportions. The standard method for this apportionment is to base the split on the income of the charity. However, you may propose other methods that are fair.

The recoverable input VAT is the total of the directly attributable input VAT and the apportioned input VAT on taxable activities.

Where a charity is undertaking a mixture of activities which fall into different categories for VAT purposes, it will need to keep detailed records of expenditure. As far as possible, expenditure needs to be related to the activity. This may mean a change to the headings in your accounting records so that they are activity based (*see chapter 10 Operational aspects, p102*).

Example: Recovering VAT on business activities

The Community Advice and Resource Centre (CARC) operates from small premises and employs several staff. They receive funding from the Legal Aid Board to provide free advice to local people. In addition, they charge for photocopying and running a payroll service. They are registered and charge VAT on all income.

Since they only have taxable business activities, they can simply identify all VAT on purchases and recover this in full.

Example: Mix of business and non-business activities

CARC (*see previous box*) are successful in a bid for grant funding for a new area of work. They will be giving free advice to members of the public. Their income excluding VAT for the coming year will be:

Legal Aid Board fees	£60,000
Photocopying and payroll service fees	£10,000
Grant	£30,000
Total	£100,000

VAT on purchases:

Photocopying	£875
Stationery	£450
Telephone	£300
Audit and legal fees	£150
General office costs	£140
Total input VAT	**£1,915**

It is not possible to directly attribute any of this input VAT to a particular activity because of the nature of the activities and the way the centre is organised. We should therefore go to the second step of apportioning the input VAT to the activities.

The standard method is based on the proportions of income:

Legal Aid Board fees	£60,000	60% business
Photocopying and payroll service fees	£10,000	10% business
Grant	£30,000	30% non-business
Total	**£100,000**	

We should therefore disallow 30% of the total input VAT. CARC can recover 70% of £1,915, i.e. £1,340.50.

PARTIAL EXEMPTION

If all business activities are exempt, then you cannot register for VAT, nor can you recover the input VAT on purchases. Any organisation undertaking a mixture of exempt and taxable activities has to check whether it is partly exempt. This may restrict the amount of input VAT which is recoverable.

Charities will be able to ignore exempt input VAT relating to incidental rental income. If this is your only exempt activity, then you do not have to check whether you are within the *de minimis* limits *see below*). Income for these purposes will be incidental if it is received passively and there is no activity to generate the income. Usually there is very little input VAT relating to low-level rental income, but you should take care in planning repairs to property if you rent it out, as this could be more substantial in some years and the input VAT may be more significant. You may then exceed the limits and the VAT will then be irrecoverable.

The partial exemption rules only apply if there is a significant amount of input VAT relating to exempt activity. If it is below *de minimis* limits then it is possible to recover all the input VAT, ignoring the fact that the organisation has some exempt supplies. The organisation is then defined as *fully taxable*.

Fully taxable status will be available if *exempt input tax* is less than £625 per month *on average* and less than 50% of total input tax. These are the *de minimis* limits.

▼ 'On average' means the average over the relevant VAT period.

▼ 'Exempt input tax' means the input VAT relating to exempt supplies, where these can be identified.

Example: Fully taxable status

Dance International stages performances, charging admission fees which are subject to VAT. They have just started to run training courses, from which they earn fee income. As a charity, they are able to treat the training course fees as exempt. Their quarterly figures showed the following:

Income net of VAT:

Admission fees	£90,000
Training fees	£10,000
Total	**£100,000**

VAT on purchases:

Photocopying	£875
Stationery	£450
Telephone	£300
Audit and legal fees	£150
General office costs	£140
Total input VAT	**£1,915**

There are no directly attributable costs of the training activity, but we have to check the partial exemption *de minimis* limits by looking at the apportioned input VAT.

Admission fees	£90,000	90%	Taxable
Training fees	£10,000	10%	Exempt
Total	**£100,000**		

Of the total input VAT, 10% relates to exempt activity. 10% of £1,915 is £191.50. The monetary limit is £625 per month or £1,875 per quarter. The exempt input VAT is below this. It also has to be less than 50% of the total input VAT. It complies with this condition too. The organisation can therefore be treated as fully taxable and recover all input VAT.

RECOVERING VAT

PARTIAL EXEMPTION CALCULATIONS

An organisation which goes above the *de minimis* limits must identify the input VAT relating to exempt and taxable activities as far as possible. The input VAT on the shared costs will be subject to a calculation to estimate the proportion which may be recovered. This will be a percentage based on the proportion of taxable supplies to total supplies.

Example: Partial exemption

Voluntary Sector Training Trust (VSTT) runs training courses as its primary activity, as well as some consultancy commissioned by clients. The training course fees are exempt from VAT as VSTT is a charity. They have registered for VAT and charge VAT on the consultancy work. Their quarterly figures showed the following:

Income net of VAT:

Training fees	£90,000
Consultancy	£10,000
Total	**£100,000**

VAT on purchases:

Freelance trainers' fees	£1,750
Freelance consultants' fees	£350
Photocopying	£875
Stationery	£450
Telephone	£300
Audit and legal fees	£150
General office costs	£140
Total input VAT	**£4,015**

Directly attributable input VAT:

Freelance trainers' fees	£1,750	exempt activity
Freelance consultants' fees	£350	taxable activity

The residual input VAT needs to be apportioned on the basis of income:

Training fees	90,000	90% exempt
Consultancy	10,000	10% taxable
Total	**£100,000**	

53

A PRACTICAL GUIDE TO VAT

> Total residual input VAT   £1,915
> £1,915 x 90% = £1,723.50   exempt
> £1,915 x 10% = £191.50   taxable
>
> **Exempt input VAT:**
>
> | | |
> |---|---|
> | Directly attributable – freelance trainers' fees | £1,750.00 |
> | Residual apportioned | £1,723.50 |
> | **Total** | **£3,473.50** |
>
> Check whether this is over the *de minimis* limit of £625 per month or £1,875 per quarter. Yes, it is over the limit. This VAT cannot therefore be recovered.
>
> Input VAT relating to taxable supplies is recoverable:
>
> | | |
> |---|---|
> | Freelance consultants' fees | £350.00 |
> | Residual apportioned | £191.50 |
> | **Total** | **£541.50** |

ANNUAL ADJUSTMENT

The rules state that you have to check for partial exemption each quarter and calculate the amount of input tax recoverable each quarter. You also have to carry out an overall calculation for the whole year, to eliminate seasonal distortions. The year in operation here is not the organisation's own financial year, but the 'tax year'. This is the year ending 31 March, or 30 April or 31 May, depending on your return date. Any differences which arise from the annual adjustment should be shown on the next VAT return as an under or over declaration of VAT. Note that such an adjustment cannot make you liable to penalties for late payment of VAT, nor does it represent an error which needs disclosure.

> ### Example: Annual adjustment
>
> VSTT (*see previous box*) builds up its consultancy work and wins a big contract in the final quarter of the tax year. Their annual figures showed the following:
>
> **Income net of VAT:**
>
> | | |
> |---|---|
> | Training fees | £350,000 |
> | Consultancy | £ 70,000 |
> | **Total** | **£420,000** |

VAT on purchases:

Freelance trainers' fees	£6,750
Freelance consultants' fees	£3,150
Photocopying	£3,800
Stationery	£1,900
Telephone	£1,400
Audit and legal fees	£ 400
General office costs	£ 560
Total input VAT	**£17,960**

Directly attributable input VAT:

Freelance trainers' fees	£6,750	exempt activity
Freelance consultants' fees	£3,150	taxable activity

The residual input VAT needs to be apportioned on the basis of income:

Training fees	£350,000	83% exempt
Consultancy	£ 70,000	17% taxable
Total	**£420,000**	
Total residual input VAT	**£8,060**	
£8,060 x 83% = £6,689.80	exempt	
£8,060 x 17% = £1,370.20	taxable	

Exempt input VAT:

Directly attributable – freelance trainers' fees	£6,750.00
Residual apportioned	£6,689.80
Total	**£13,439.80**

Check whether this is over the *de minimis* limit of £625 per month or £7,500 per annum. Yes, it is over the limit. This VAT cannot therefore be recovered.

Input VAT relating to taxable supplies is recoverable:

Freelance consultants' fees	£3,150.00
Residual apportioned	£1,370.20
Total	**£4,520.20**

You then add together the recovered input VAT on the four quarterly returns already submitted. Compare this total to the input VAT relating to taxable supplies calculated on an annual basis. The difference should be included in the input VAT figure on the next quarterly return.

A PRACTICAL GUIDE TO VAT

CHARITIES WITH NON-BUSINESS AND EXEMPT ACTIVITIES

It is actually quite common for charities to have activities that fall into all the VAT categories. The calculations therefore have to first exclude the VAT on purchases relating to non-business activities, then check whether partial exemption applies and calculate the recoverable VAT accordingly.

Example: Mix of non-business, exempt and taxable activities

ABC Charity promotes awareness of a condition by disseminating free information, selling some publications. Their quarterly figures showed the following:

Income:

Grants and donations	£175,000
Sales of publications	£20,000
Fundraising events	£15,000
Total	**£210,000**

VAT on purchases:

Directly attributable to publications	£875
Directly attributable to fundraising events	£ 634
Residual VAT	£7,241
Total	**£8,750**

Step 1 *Identify the VAT categories of income*

Grants and donations	£175,000	83%	non-business
Sales of publications	£20,000	10%	zero-rated
Fundraising events	£15,000	7%	exempt
Total	**£210,000**		

Step 2 *Apportion the residual VAT*

Non-business	83%	£6,010
Zero-rated	10%	£724
Exempt	7%	£507
Total		**£7,241**

Step 3 *Summary of VAT on purchases by categories*

	Direct	Residual	Total
Non-business	-	£6,010	£6,010
Zero-rated	£875	£724	£1,599
Exempt	£634	£507	£1,141
			£8,750

Step 4 *Check partial exemption* de minimis *rules*

Exempt input VAT is £1,141. Is this below the quarterly limit of £1,875? Yes.

Is exempt input VAT less than 50% of total input VAT? Yes, total input VAT is only the business VAT, which is the element relating to the zero-rated and exempt activities totalling £2,740, of which 50% is £1,370.

Step 5 *Summarise recoverable VAT*

ABC Charity can be treated as fully taxable in respect of its business activities as it is below the *de minimis* limits this quarter. However, none of the VAT relating to the non-business activities can be recovered.

Recoverable VAT:

	Direct	Residual	Total
Zero-rated	£875	£724	£1,599
Exempt	£634	£507	£1,141
			£2,740

ABC Charity can recover £2,740, representing approximately 31% of the total VAT incurred on purchases. This is actually quite good, given that 83% of its income is non-business. However, this is fair, as the main cost of the non-business activity is staff salaries, on which there is no VAT. ABC Charity will have to do an annual adjustment to check the overall recovery.

METHODS OF CALCULATING RECOVERABLE VAT

Charities should adopt a method for calculating the recoverable VAT that is fair. The basic method they have to use involves the direct attribution of input VAT to activities and then the apportionment of residual VAT on a fair basis.

Charities should therefore attempt as far as possible to identify the input VAT directly attributable to their activities. Usually, charities use the VAT coding system of computerised accounting systems to achieve this (*see chapter 10 Operational aspects, p102*). In nearly all cases, you will be able to increase the amount of VAT you recover by undertaking this task thoroughly. The residual input VAT subject to the apportionment calculation is then lower.

The basis for the apportionment of the residual input VAT is income if you use the standard method. However, Customs & Excise will consider other methods, as long as they produce a fair result. Methods commonly used involve using proportions based on:

A PRACTICAL GUIDE TO VAT

- ▼ staff numbers;
- ▼ staff salaries;
- ▼ staff time;
- ▼ staff and volunteer time;
- ▼ floor area occupied by divisions of the organisation.

The method has to be independently verifiable, rather than based on a subjective judgement. There should be a formula and some methods will require proper record keeping, for example if you wish to base the method on the staff time spent on different activities.

You should write to your VAT office proposing a method. Once agreement has been reached on the method, a 'contract' will be issued by Customs & Excise setting out the method in detail. You should continue to use the old method until you receive agreement to the new special method. Once this has been agreed, the method should be used for at least two years before it is revised again, unless there is a significant change in circumstances.

If your circumstances change and this will affect the method, you should contact your VAT office. You do not have to notify the VAT office if the calculation simply produces a different percentage. They only need to be told of changes that affect the principle behind the method. For example, a merger with another charity would be a significant change, or if the charity moved premises and the old method had been based on proportions of floor space.

Example: Apportionment of residual VAT by special method

ABC Charity wish to consider other options for calculating their recoverable VAT. They consider staff the most important driver behind the charity's work and so they propose to use staff salaries as the most fair basis on which to apportion residual VAT.

Staff salaries for the quarter were:

Relating to non-business activities	£28,450
Relating to publications sales	£7,500
Relating to fundraising events	£6,200
	£42,150
Relating to overall management and administration	£12,340
Total	**£54,490**

The salaries relating to overall management and administration can be spread over the other activities in proportion to their relative size. These then give us the proportions to apply to the residual VAT by calculating the relative salary cost compared to the total salary cost.

	Salary	Mgt & Admin	Total	%
Non-business	£28,450	£8,329	£36,779	67%
Publications	£ 7,500	£2,196	£ 9,696	18%
Fundraising events	£6,200	£1,815	£8,015	15%
Total	**£42,150**	**£12,340**	**£54,490**	

Recalculating the apportionment of residual VAT in **Step 2** of the previous example on this basis:

Non-business	67%	£4,852
Zero-rated	18%	£1,303
Exempt	15%	£1,086
		£7,241

This changes the amounts shown in **Step 3**:

	Direct	Residual	Total
Non-business	–	£4,852	£4,852
Zero-rated	£875	£1,303	£2,178
Exempt	£634	£1,086	£1,720
			£8,750

We have to once again check the partial exemption *de minimis* rules as in **Step 4**

Exempt input VAT is £1,720. Is this below the quarterly limit of £1,875? Yes.

Is exempt input VAT less than 50% of total input VAT? Yes, total input VAT is only the business VAT, which is the element relating to the zero-rated and exempt activities totalling £3,898 of which 50% is £1,949.

The total amount recoverable is therefore:

	Direct	Residual	Total
Zero-rated	£875	£1,303	£2,178
Exempt	£634	£1,086	£1,720
			£3,898

Under the special method ABC Charity can recover £3,898, representing nearly 45% of their total VAT on purchases. This is higher than under the standard method, so it would be worthwhile agreeing the method with Customs & Excise.

PROVISIONAL RECOVERY RATE

As it can be a lengthy process to calculate the amount of VAT recoverable by the full method each quarter, Customs & Excise are prepared to agree a provisional rate of recovery. This would probably be agreed after a period of registration, say one year. The first annual adjustment would calculate the recovery rate for the past year. This rate could then be used on a provisional basis for the coming year. The annual adjustment calculation would ensure that the correct amount of VAT is recovered overall for the year and then provide the new figure for the provisional basis of recovery calculations on VAT returns in the coming year.

A change in the provisional recovery rate does not represent a change in the partial exemption method.

6 ▾ Saving VAT

This chapter looks at ways in which charities can save VAT when buying goods and services. In particular, charities can buy certain goods and services at the zero rate of VAT. In addition there are a few situations where goods or services can be treated as exempt or outside the scope of VAT, thus saving VAT on purchases.

ZERO-RATING

There is a very significant benefit to charities if the goods which they are buying can be zero-rated. It means that the goods or services are cheaper to the charity; it is an immediate tax relief as there is no reclaiming to do and so it does not cause cashflow complications. It is an effective relief from the government's point of view because it can be specifically targeted at particular needs or particular people. It is available to all charities, large or small, whether registered for VAT or not. It is a relief without any complications; there is no need to consider whether the supply is business or non-business; there is very little administration involved.

There is quite a long list of items which can be supplied at the zero rate of VAT when supplied to a charity. The list has been added to over a number of years and various bodies have been successful in their lobbying to get this relief extended. This particular form of relief is in danger of being abolished when the UK harmonises its VAT regime with Europe.

Zero-rating on purchases is available both to charities registered for VAT and to those which are not registered.

In most situations, the charity should provide a certified declaration to the supplier to enable the supplier to charge VAT at zero rate. The supplier must be registered for VAT.

In addition there are some goods and services which are zero-rated for any purchaser, mainly relating to printed matter.

OTHER SAVINGS

There are a few situations where a charity can save VAT because a supply can be exempt in certain circumstances, such as agency nursing staff. Alternatively, a lower rate of VAT may apply, such as fuel and power. These situations are also covered below.

GOODS AND SERVICES ELIGIBLE FOR VAT SAVINGS

Listed below, in alphabetical order, are the specific goods and services covered in this chapter.

- ▼ Advertising
- ▼ Aids for disabled people
- ▼ Ambulances
- ▼ Boats for disabled people
- ▼ Collecting tins and badges
- ▼ Conferences and training
- ▼ Construction of new buildings
- ▼ Direct mail
- ▼ Disabled access
- ▼ Emergency alarm systems
- ▼ Fuel and power
- ▼ Hearing aids
- ▼ Imports
- ▼ Lifeboats
- ▼ Medical equipment and supplies
- ▼ Medicines
- ▼ Motability scheme
- ▼ Nursing staff
- ▼ Printed matter
- ▼ Rescue equipment
- ▼ Talking books for the blind
- ▼ Vehicles
- ▼ Visual aids for the partially sighted
- ▼ Wireless sets for the blind

ADVERTISING

Charities can buy advertising and closely related services at zero rate VAT. Initially, the scope of this relief was restricted to newspaper advertising and to the actual cost of the advertisement. The zero-rating has since been extended to include advertisements in all media and all preparation work, such as design and artwork. In addition, the advertisement no longer has to be specifically for the purpose of raising money or making known the objects of the charity. The effective date of the changes was 1 April 2000.

In order to zero rate the invoice, the supplier must be satisfied that it is a supply of advertising to a charity. Where the charity is claiming the zero-rating for goods that are closely related to the design or production of an advertisement, then the charity must give the supplier a declaration that the advertisement is for a relevant purpose. The supplier may need to check their action with their local VAT office, because if they make a mistake, they will have to account for the VAT.

The zero-rating applies to all types of advertising by charities, including recruitment advertisements, attracting new members, pupils or students, advertising events, raising awareness or fundraising.

All media are allowed, including badges, balloons, banners, carrier bags, cinema, TV and radio advertisements, clothing, flags, internet advertising (except for adverts on the charity's own website), all types of printed matter including business cards, calendars, car parking tickets, diaries, greetings cards, lottery tickets, posters, stationery. However, note that it is not the whole item which qualifies for zero-rating – it is only the purchase of advertising space on these media. Thus, the purchase of lottery tickets for the charity's own use, for example, does not fall within the zero-rating.

Zero-rating is not available in the following cases:

▼ personally addressed letters and other targeted fundraising activities. Direct marketing and telesales cannot therefore be zero-rated. It may be possible for individual items of the promotional material used to be zero-rated (*see also the section on Direct mail, p67*);

▼ advertising on the charity's own website, nor the creation of the charity's own website, even if the website is being used to raise funds;

▼ where the charity prepares its own advertisements in house;

▼ where the supply is not directly to a charity, for example where the supply is to a trading subsidiary;

▼ where the advertisement appears in a charity's own magazine, notice board, calendar or other publication.

AIDS FOR DISABLED PEOPLE

Certain specialised goods and services needed by disabled people are zero-rated. A disabled person is defined in law to mean chronically sick or disabled (included in the Chronically Sick and Disabled Persons Act 1970). This includes people who are blind, deaf or dumb; substantially and permanently handicapped by illness, injury or congenital deformity. The zero-rating in this section relates to goods for use by a specific disabled person, whether purchased by the disabled person or by a charity on their behalf.

A separate piece of legislation also permits non-profit-making hospitals and research institutions and charities caring for disabled people to obtain the same relief if the aids are bought from charitable funds or are being donated.

The following goods are covered:

▼ medical or surgical appliances designed solely for the relief of a severe abnormality or severe injury. The appliances included are special clothing or footwear and wigs, renal haemodialysis units, oxygen concentrators, artificial respirators, TENS machines and other similar apparatus (*see VAT Notice 701/7 for further details*);

▼ electrically or mechanically adjustable beds designed for invalids;

▼ commode chairs and stools, devices incorporating a bidet jet and warm air drier and frames or other devices for sitting over or rising from sanitary appliances;

▼ chair or stair lifts designed for use in connection with invalid wheelchairs, although these can be used by the person out of the wheelchair;

▼ hoists and lifters designed for use by invalids;

▼ motor vehicles designed or substantially and permanently adapted for the carriage of a disabled person in a wheelchair or on a stretcher and of no more than five other persons. The vehicle should be large enough in each case for the disabled person to be accommodated comfortably. For use by a person in a wheelchair, it should have a hoist or ramp to enable a person to embark and disembark while sitting in the wheelchair. In order to obtain zero-rating of the whole vehicle, the charity or individual should arrange for the conversion work to be carried out before they purchase the vehicle. Any new vehicle meeting these conditions will also qualify for relief from car tax (but not Road Fund Licence). In order to obtain the VAT and tax relief, you must arrange for Customs & Excise to inspect the vehicle. Ask your supplier to contact their local VAT office to arrange the inspection before you take delivery;

▼ other equipment and appliances designed solely for use by a disabled person, including wheelchairs. General purpose goods are not eligible, even if they are being used by a disabled person. Customs & Excise will consider the intention of the supplier in designing and marketing the product in assessing whether the goods were designed solely for use by a disabled person. The fact that an item may be used by able-bodied persons does not mean that it does not qualify for zero-rating.

Note that some goods will not qualify for zero-rating, even if the supply is to a disabled person. An example of this would be the provision of shoes to someone whose disability does not mean that they need special surgical footwear. Since spectacles, hearing aids and dentures are normally standard rated, there can be situations where VAT is being paid on these goods for disabled people.

Goods that have to be standard-rated:

▼ air conditioning units;

▼ asthma, hay fever and allergy products, including special filters for vacuum cleaners and the like;

▼ carpets;

▼ computers – only specialist items may be zero-rated, even when the computer is sold as a package;

▼ golf buggies;

▼ hearing aids.

Note that if the items qualify for zero-rating, then parts and accessories necessary for the goods are included in the zero-rating, as is the repair and maintenance of such goods.

AMBULANCES

Emergency vehicles of all types may be purchased at zero rate when bought out of donated goods by an eligible body (*see the section on Medical equipment, p69, for definition of an eligible body*). To qualify they should be used for transporting sick or injured people or animals and must comply with the following conditions. They must have:

▼ permanent signs on the front and both sides identifying them as ambulances;

▼ adequate doorspace for the loading of a patient on a stretcher;

▼ seating in the back for an attendant;

▼ a proper stretcher as part of the equipment.

(*See VAT Notice 701/6.*)

BOATS FOR DISABLED PEOPLE

Boats that have been designed or substantially and permanently adapted for use by disabled people will qualify for zero-rating. To qualify, the boat should allow for the embarkation of disabled people in wheelchairs and their movement about the boat, as well as have wheelchair clamps. It should have special toilet and washing facilities and may have sleeping, galley and steering facilities for use by disabled people.

COLLECTING TINS AND BADGES

Customs & Excise introduced a new concession from 1 April 2000 to enable charities to buy many forms of collecting tins at the zero rate. The concession includes the following items:

▼ all forms of collecting boxes, providing they are tamper-proof (capable of being sealed) and specifically designed for collecting money for charity. They should bear the charity name by indelible printing, embossing or having raised letters. The zero-rating applies to small collecting boxes carried by collectors or the static boxes. They may incorporate a device such as a balance or helter skelter mechanism;

▼ collecting envelopes used for house to house collections or in church collections;

▼ pre-printed letters appealing solely for money for the charity;

▼ envelopes used with appeal letters for sending in a donation, providing they are overprinted with an appeal request related to that contained in the letter;

▼ lapel stickers and badges given free as an acknowledgement to donors which have a nominal value. Badges or other tokens given in return of an anticipated donation of £1 are considered to be of nominal value. The cost to the charity would therefore be considerably less than £1. Included are small items such as paper stickers, ribbons, artificial flowers where these are the emblem for the charity and metal badges, subject to the minimal cost criteria.

Excluded are:

▼ elaborate boxes which have an additional purpose, such as a game or a quiz machine;

▼ general purpose buckets, although special lids designed to seal standard buckets may qualify for the zero-rating;

▼ appeal letters that incorporate a survey or questionnaire.

CONFERENCES AND TRAINING

If your charity organises conferences and training, it may be able to save VAT on the conference services it buys in. A conference or training course will usually qualify as exempt vocational training if it is training, re-training or the provision of work experience for any trade, profession or employment; or for any voluntary work of a charitable nature (including education, health, safety or welfare). The net is cast widely and vocational training will apply to courses, conferences, lectures, workshops and seminars. The training can be for those already in work, where the intention is to improve their knowledge in order to improve their performance in work, or to prepare people for future work.

If you organise the conference or training so that it takes place at a venue that is an educational establishment, then you can buy the accommodation and catering as an exempt supply. Note that for this exemption to apply, there has to be a charge for the event and your charity has to be an 'eligible body', that is a not-for-profit body supplying education and training (*see also the section on Education in chapter 3 Activities of charities, p27*). (*See VAT Notice 701/30, para 6.4.*)

CONSTRUCTION OF NEW BUILDiNGS

The construction of new buildings for residential use or *relevant charitable* use will be zero-rated. Relevant charitable use generally refers to the non-business activities of charities, as well as residential buildings. For more details of this complex area, *see chapter 8 Property, p82*.

DIRECT MAIL

The services of direct mail agents will normally be standard-rated, but elements of the service can be zero-rated. The actual contents of the package being mailed out may be zero-rated, depending on the nature of the material. Where a package consists of several items but one item has far more significance than the others (for example a leaflet and a form for completion) then the most significant item determines the VAT category of the whole package.

Where the items in a package all have similar significance (for example an appeal letter, a pen, a survey form and a pre-printed envelope), then the liability of the whole package should be determined by the VAT category of the majority of the items, ignoring the outer envelope. Where this is problematic, the VAT category of the most expensive items should be the category to apply to the whole package. (*See VAT Notice 701/10.*)

Some elements of the package may be zero-rated because they fall within the rules for charity advertising.

A direct mail agent can exempt the supply of postage services providing they are acting as the charity's agent and only charge the actual cost of postage. The charity should be able to specify the recipients of the mail shot or have access to the names and addresses prior to despatch.

The agent's fee for providing the service will be standard-rated. Where charities use agents for direct mail, they should ensure that the services are split and VAT applied correctly to the various elements. If the direct mail agent invoices for one overall supply of services, then VAT at standard rate would apply to the whole amount. Note that it is only charities that can purchase advertising materials at zero rate VAT, so the charity should purchase qualifying envelopes and letters direct and pass these on to the agent for distribution.

If charities organise their own direct mail activities, then they should be able to buy in much of the printed materials at zero rate, either because of the printed matter rules or because they qualify for zero-rating as charity advertising. However, personalised letters do not qualify for zero-rating under the charity advertising rules (since 1 April 2000).

DISABLED ACCESS

The conversion of a disabled person's home, and work such as the widening of door-ways, building of ramps, installation of lifts and specially adapted toilets, is all zero-rated. So is the repair and maintenance of any equipment and any incidental building or preparation work. The zero-rating also applies to residential homes or day centres for the disabled. A charity may obtain the zero-rating for building and for the provision of toilet facilities for the disabled in a charity-run building used for chari-table purposes.

Kitchen furniture fitted into a kitchen in the course of construction of a new dwelling may be zero-rated under normal construction rules. For existing kitchens, items must be solely designed for disabled people, for example when made to the specification of a disabled person, if they are to be zero-rated.

Other alterations to buildings are not covered and are standard rated. This is still the case even if a kitchen or bedroom has to be adapted to suit a disabled person.

EMERGENCY ALARM SYSTEMS

The alarm system must be capable of operation by a disabled person and be set up to enable him or her to alert directly a specified person, such as a warden, or a control centre. The zero-rating is available on purchases by a disabled person or by a charity for onward supply to a disabled person. The zero-rating is extended to the supply of services necessarily performed by a control centre in receiving and responding to calls.

FUEL AND POWER

Charities can pay the reduced rate of 5% on fuel and power supplies used for residential or non-business charitable purposes. If the building has mixed use, then the lower rate can apply to the whole providing at least 60% of the building is used for a qualifying purpose. If the proportion is lower, then there has to be an apportionment and the lower rate will only apply to the non-business element.

HEARING AIDS

Generally, hearing aids are not within the zero-rating relief and the majority of people have to pay standard rate VAT on the purchase of hearing aids.

However, specialist devices designed for the auditory training of deaf children are zero-rated, as are special harnesses designed solely for use by deaf children when using the training device. Other specialised aids designed for people with severely defective hearing but which are not hearing aids as such are zero-rated. Such aids include TV hearing aids, induction loop systems and tinnitus maskers.

IMPORTS

Goods that would qualify for zero-rating if supplied in the UK can be zero-rated if imported. A zero-rating certificate needs to be produced to the import agent.

LIFEBOATS

The supply, repair and maintenance of any vessel made direct to a charity providing rescue or assistance at sea is zero-rated. Also included is the supply of tractors, winching equipment and the construction and repair of slipways. In addition repairs, maintenance, spares and accessories are zero-rated.

MEDICAL EQUIPMENT

The purchase of certain items out of donated funds by a charity or other eligible body will be zero-rated. There are fairly stringent conditions for the zero-rating to apply, although there is some overlap with the zero-rating of aids for disabled people (*see above*).

The goods which are covered are medical equipment to be used in the diagnosis or treatment of patients. This excludes more general use items which may be necessary in a hospital or nursing home. It can include computer equipment, video equipment, sterilising equipment, goods designed for use in a laboratory and refrigeration equipment. There are a number of exceptions including equipment such as air conditioning, smoke alarms and waste disposal units.

Repair and maintenance of all such goods is also covered by the zero-rating.

An eligible body includes:

▼ health authority or health trust;

▼ not-for-profit hospitals;

▼ registered care home;

▼ rescue and first aid charities;

▼ charities providing care or medical or surgical treatment for disabled people either in a residential care home, daycentre (not one providing primarily social or recreational activities) or in their own homes;

▼ charities whose sole purpose is to provide transport to disabled people, by concession.

(*See VAT Notice 701/6.*)

MEDICINES

Medicines are zero-rated when supplied to a charity looking after humans or animals or undertaking medical research. This applies to all substances used in the treatment or diagnosis of illness or for the prevention of illness. It includes anaesthetics, vaccines, contraception and the ingredients for making medicines. Any substances used directly in medical research are also zero-rated, although this relief only applies to charities actually engaged in medical research. This applies equally to veterinary research.

MOTABILITY SCHEME

The lease of vehicles, whether or not specially adapted for use by a disabled person, are zero-rated when let under the Motability scheme. The subsequent sale of vehicles at the end of the lease is also zero-rated.

NURSING STAFF

Agencies supplying nursing staff may be able to exempt part or all of the supply. If the agency employs the nurse, then the whole invoice to the organisation is exempt. If the agency is acting on behalf of the organisation in paying the nurse (who is the employee of the organisation) then VAT does have to be charged on the agent's fee, but the reimbursement of salary is exempt. The exemption can only apply to registered or enrolled nurses and midwives.

PRINTED MATTER

The zero-rating of many printed materials is not a concession to charities, but applies to all supplies. Printed materials will generally be zero-rated where their primary purpose is to convey information:

- books and booklets;
- brochures and pamphlets;
- leaflets;
- newspapers;
- journals and periodicals;
- children's picture books;
- children's painting books;
- music (printed, duplicated or manuscript);
- maps, charts and topographical plans.

It is the nature of the item, not the method of production, which determines whether it is zero-rated. For example, a newsletter produced by photocopying would still qualify for zero-rating. However, publishing by electronic means does not fall within the zero-rating, nor do cassettes and video tapes.

A leaflet has to be a single sheet not larger than A4 and primarily intended to be held in the hand for reading by individuals (rather than for hanging up for general display). It has to convey information and be complete in itself. It should contain a significant proportion of text and at least 50 copies should be produced so that it can be generally distributed. A leaflet may also be up to A2 in size provided it is printed on both sides, folded down to A4 size or smaller and meets all the other conditions.

A 'significant proportion of text' is further defined: less than 25% of the total printed area should be for writing on. If you incorporate a detachable reply coupon or similar, then this would have to be less than 25% of the total leaflet. If you design a leaflet where the whole sheet has to be returned after some part of it is completed, then this makes the whole thing standard-rated.

In addition, the leaflet should be on paper, not card. Menus and cookery cards, cassette inlay cards and any laminated products are standard-rated.

Printed items that will not be zero-rated, but standard-rated include:

- posters;
- diaries and calendars;
- stationery;

A PRACTICAL GUIDE TO VAT

▼ postcards and greeting cards;

▼ material designed to be filled in, such as record books, notebooks, school work-books, exercise books. Where workbooks are in a question and answer format, the spaces left for the answers are deemed to be incidental and therefore the book can still be zero-rated.

These items may qualify for zero-rating as advertising materials (*see the section on Advertising, p63*).

A printer with a contract to supply goods which qualify for zero-rating may zero rate any preparation work, such as design and typesetting, and any post-production work, such as folding, inserting into envelopes or wrapping. It is therefore a considerable advantage to charities to arrange for all services to be bought in by the printer and then invoiced to the charity as one zero-rated supply. (*See VAT Notice 701/10.*)

Example certificate to obtain zero-rating on charity advertising

[To be prepared on charity's letterhead and sent to the supplier at the time of placing the order.]

To: [Name of supplier]

[Address of supplier]

Charity advertising

I   [full name]

[status in the charity]

of   [name and address of charity]

declare that the above named charity is buying from/importing from

[name of supplier]

the following goods or services eligible for relief from VAT under item 8 of Zero Rate Group 15

[insert description of goods or services]

Signature

Date

You should retain this certificate for production to your VAT office. The production of this certificate does not authorise the zero-rating of the equipment. It is your responsibility to ensure that the goods or services supplied are eligible before zero-rating them.

RESCUE EQUIPMENT

This covers specialist equipment needed by search and rescue teams such as heat detecting equipment and image intensifiers. Such equipment will be zero-rated only when supplied to a charity which provides rescue and first aid services. General items such as mobile phones and binoculars are not eligible for the zero-rating.

Example certificate to obtain zero-rating on disabled access

[To be prepared on charity's letterhead and sent to the supplier at the time of placing the order.]

To: [name of supplier]

       [address of supplier]

Disabled access

I   [full name]

                                                       [status in the charity]

of   [name and address of charity]

declare that the above named charity is buying from [name of supplier]

▼ services for the purpose of facilitating a disabled person's entry to and movement within the charity's building and

▼ services of providing a washroom/lavatory for use by disabled persons in a building used principally by a charity for charitable purposes and I claim that the supply of these goods or services is eligible for relief from VAT under Group 12 of Schedule 8 of the VAT Act 1994.

                                       Signature

                                       Date

You should retain this certificate for production to your VAT office. The production of this certificate does not authorise the zero-rating of the equipment. It is your responsibility to ensure that the goods or services supplied are eligible before zero-rating them.

There are severe penalties for making a false declaration. If you are in any doubt about the eligibility of the goods or services you are buying, you should seek advice from your local VAT office before signing either of these declarations.

TALKING BOOKS FOR THE BLIND

Charities working with blind people may buy certain supplies at zero rate VAT. These include sound recording equipment and parts and accessories for making tape recordings for use by the visually impaired. Radios and cassette recorders supplied to charities for free loan or rental to blind people are also included in the relief provisions and may be zero-rated. Evidence must be given to the supplier that the goods are to be used in accordance with the conditions above. A declaration should be given to the supplier confirming this, which the supplier must retain for its records.

VEHICLES

Zero-rating applies to vehicles purchased out of donated funds when supplied to an eligible body (*see the section on Medical equipment, p69*). The following are included:

▼ vehicles which have been specifically designed or adapted to carry one or more handicapped people in wheelchairs. These will have no more than 50 seats and will have a certain proportion of wheelchair spaces; at least two wheelchair spaces for vehicles with 17 to 26 seats; at least three spaces for vehicles with 27 to 36 seats; at least four spaces for vehicles with 37 to 46 seats; at least five spaces for vehicles with more than 47 seats. There must be either a fitted electrically or hydraulically operated lift, or if the vehicle has less than 17 seats, a fitted ramp to provide access for a passenger in a wheelchair;

▼ unadapted motor vehicles with more than 6 seats but fewer than 51 seats for use by charities and other eligible bodies providing care for the blind, deaf or mentally handicapped or terminally ill people and used mainly for their transportation.

(*See notes on the case Help the Aged under Summaries of useful VAT cases.*)

VISUAL AIDS FOR THE PARTIALLY SIGHTED

Spectacles and contact lenses cannot be zero-rated, however special low vision aids will qualify for zero-rating. Included are custom-made spectacle-mounted low vision aids and closed circuit video magnification systems capable of magnifying text and images.

WIRELESS SETS FOR BLIND PEOPLE

Radios and tape players bought by a charity for free loan or rental to blind people will be zero-rated.

7 ▼ International aspects of VAT

This chapter looks at the VAT rules applicable to transactions where there is an international dimension. This can apply to the importation of goods as well as exporting goods. Services which cross borders can have complex rules about where they are deemed to be supplied, with a different set of rules applying when the activity is in the European Community.

GOODS

Generally, goods supplied in the UK will be subject to UK VAT law. Where the place of supply of goods is outside the UK, then there is no UK VAT liability. However, a UK supplier who makes supplies in another European Community (EC) country may be liable to register there, subject to the registration rules in that country. Similarly, a business which is based outside the UK may have to register for VAT in the UK if the place of supply of the goods is in the UK. (*See the section on Distance selling, p79, for rules on distance sales.*)

SERVICES

Services are treated differently to goods, mainly because it is more difficult to establish where the supply of a service takes place. There are complex 'place of supply' rules. Broadly, a service is subject to UK VAT if the supplier of the service has a place of business in the UK. The exceptions to this general rule are:

▼ services relating to land, as the place of supply will be determined by the location of the land. This includes building works and professional fees;

▼ services in connection with exhibitions and conferences, because they are supplied where they are physically carried out. This includes cultural, artistic, sporting, scientific and educational events or entertainment, as well as exhibitions, conferences and meetings. Ancillary services to the main supply are included;

▼ certain services relating to intellectual property and intangible assets. The services included under this category are:

- transfers of intellectual property rights such as patents, copyrights, trademarks and licences to use intellectual property;

- advertising services;

- services of consultants, engineers, lawyers, accountants and other professionals, and data processing. These may include research, interpreting, writing software, but not secretarial services;

- the provision of information, including on-line information;

- banking and financial services;

- secondment of staff (but not the provision of services);

- provision of telecommunication services including internet services;

- services such as travel arrangements and accommodation that fall within the tour operators' margin scheme (TOMS, *see the section on Challenge events in chapter 4, p43*), for which there are special arrangements.

Establishing the place of supply of a service is important as this determines whether you should charge VAT on it or not. If you are supplying a service that falls within the exceptions quoted above, such as intellectual property, to someone outside the EC then the supply falls outside the scope of UK VAT.

If the recipient of any of the above services is an individual in the EC, then the place of supply is the UK and VAT has to be charged as normal. The supply can be made without charging VAT if the recipient is a business in the EC, although you have to obtain the VAT registration number of that business and quote it on the invoice.

Supplies under the tour operators' margin scheme are zero-rated when the holiday is enjoyed outside the EC, standard-rated when enjoyed within the EC.

EXPORTING TO COUNTRIES OUTSIDE THE EC

An export of goods from the UK to a destination outside the EC is zero-rated. Evidence of despatch and therefore exportation must be retained.

Export of any goods by a charity is zero-rated. The export is treated as a business activity, even though the goods may be distributed for free as part of the charitable activities. This enables the charity to recover VAT on the purchases and overheads related to the export.

IMPORTING FROM OUTSIDE THE EC

VAT is charged and payable on the importation of goods into the UK from outside the EC. It is treated in a similar way to customs duty, although it is in addition to any customs or excise duty payable. The rate of VAT applicable is determined under the normal rules and is payable whether the importer is VAT-registered or not.

Charities may import certain goods free of VAT:

▼ basic necessities such as food, medicines, clothing, blankets, medical aids which are required to meet a person's immediate needs obtained without charge for free distribution to the needy by a *relevant organisation*. A relevant organisation is a public body or charitable or philanthropic organisation;

▼ donated medical equipment;

▼ goods for use by a disabled person or obtained by a charity for use by disabled people;

▼ goods donated by overseas bodies for fundraising events;

▼ office equipment donated by overseas organisations;

▼ goods for free distribution in disaster relief in an EC country where authorisation has been given by the European Commission;

▼ goods donated to charities working with disabled people, where the goods will be used in their education, employment or social advancement. Additionally, spare parts and accessories related to those goods will fall within the exemption.

Excluded are alcoholic beverages, tobacco products, coffee, tea and motor vehicles other than ambulances. Additionally, there must be no commercial use.

A declaration must be signed and lodged with the import entry declaration made to Customs & Excise at the port or airport of importation. (*See VAT Notice 317 for further information.*)

Organisations which are VAT registered and will be importing goods should apply for a Trader's Unique Reference Number (TURN) to enable them to reclaim VAT paid on imports. This can be obtained by writing to:

TURN Team T & SO 6
Room 904, Portcullis House
Victoria Avenue
Southend-on-Sea
SS2 6AL
Tel: 01702 366425/27

TRANSACTIONS BETWEEN EC MEMBER STATES

Supplies of goods between countries in the EC are not regarded as imports and exports, but as 'acquisitions' and 'supplies'. We are still in a transitional phase while a definitive system for the operation of VAT across the whole EC is introduced. The final scheme will be based on the principle that goods and services should be taxed in the country of origin.

ACQUISITIONS

If you are registered for VAT and you buy goods from another country in the EC, then you must account for the output VAT on the acquisition on your next VAT return. The rate applicable is based on the UK rules. So if the goods would be zero-rated in the UK, then they are zero-rated as an acquisition. You may also claim back this VAT as input tax, subject to any partial exemption calculations you would normally make. Thus you enter the VAT as both output and input VAT. For example, you purchase some equipment in Belgium. You have provided the supplier with your UK VAT number and so have not been charged VAT on the purchase in Belgium. You must show the acquisition on your VAT return and add the VAT due onto your normal output VAT. You may also claim back this amount of VAT as normal input VAT on a purchase.

If you sell to customers in the EC who are not registered for VAT, then you charge VAT at the normal rate applying to those goods and services in the UK. However, you will need to check the distance selling rules if the volumes get above a certain limit (*see the section on Distance selling, p79*).

If you sell to customers in the EC who are registered for VAT, then you zero-rate the sale, but you must quote the customer's VAT number on the invoice.

AIDS FOR DISABLED PEOPLE

Goods acquired from EC countries that qualify for zero-rating in the UK will not necessarily be free of VAT when brought into the UK. Individuals and charities which are not registered for VAT will not be able to recover the VAT suffered in another EC country. VAT registered charities, however, have to account for VAT on acquisitions from other EC countries as output VAT on their VAT return, rather than paying the VAT in the country of origin. Goods qualifying for the zero-rating can be included on the VAT return at zero rate.

Countries in the European Community

Austria

Belgium

Denmark (not the Faroe Islands and Greenland)

Finland (not the Aland Islands)

France (including Monaco but not including Martinique, French Guyana, Guadeloupe, Reunion and St Pierre and Miquelon)

Germany (not Busingen and the Isle of Heligoland but including Jungholz and Mittelberg)

Greece (not Mount Athos – Agion Poros)

Eire (the Republic of Ireland)

Italy (not the communes of Livigno and Campione d'Italia and the Italian waters of Lake Lugano)

Luxembourg

Netherlands

Portugal (including the Azores and Madeira)

Spain (including the Balearic Islands but not the Canary Islands, Ceuta and Melilla)

Sweden

United Kingdom (including the Isle of Man but not the Channel Islands or Gibraltar)

DISTANCE SELLING

Sales to non-VAT registered individuals may count as distance selling if a certain threshold is exceeded. You must then register for VAT in that EC country (or appoint a tax representative to act for you). You will no longer charge VAT in the UK, but charge VAT at the applicable rate in the country of destination of the goods.

Each EC country has the option of applying a distance selling threshold of either €35,000 or €100,000 per calendar year (or the equivalent in local currency).

Countries adopting a threshold of €100,000:

Austria

France

Germany

Luxembourg

Netherlands

UK

Countries adopting a threshold of €35,000:

Belgium

Denmark

Finland

Greece

Ireland

Italy

Portugal

Spain

Sweden

VOLUNTARY REGISTRATION

You may choose to register in another EC country before reaching the distance-selling threshold. You need to notify your local VAT office not less than 30 days before the first supply will be made under the new registration. Notification needs to be in writing and advise the country or countries to which the distance selling registration relates. You also have to send your VAT office a copy of the application for registration in the other EC country or countries (or certificates of registration) within 30 days of the first supply.

Once registered on a voluntary basis, you have to stay registered for two full calendar years before you can cancel the registration.

Once registered, you have to follow the local rules for submitting returns. You will also include the value of invoiced sales in boxes 6 and 8 on the VAT return.

RECOVERING VAT ON PURCHASES IN ANOTHER EC COUNTRY

If you are not registered for VAT in another EC country, but suffer VAT on goods or services purchased in that country, then you can apply for the VAT to be refunded to you.

In order to obtain a refund you must not be selling goods and services in that country, but you must have acquired the goods or services for a business activity. You have to submit an application form to the relevant authority in that country in the language of that country, attaching original invoices.

You also have to produce a certificate of status (valid for one year) issued by Customs & Excise stating that you are a taxable person, give a written declaration that no goods or services have been supplied in the EC country and undertake to repay any amounts reclaimed in error.

(*For more information see VAT Notice 723.*)

What VAT is called in other EC countries

Country	Name	Abbreviation
Austria	Mehrwertsteuer	Mwst
Belgium	Taxe sur la Valeur Ajoutée	TVA
	Belasting over de Toegevoegde Waarde	BTW
Denmark	Omsaetningafgift	
Finland	Arvonlisavero	ALV
France	Taxe sur la Valeur Ajoutée	TVA
Germany	Mehrwertsteuer	Mwst
Greece	Arithmos Forologikou Mitroou	FPA
Ireland	Value Added Tax	VAT
Italy	Imposta sul Valore Aggiunto	IVA
Luxembourg	Taxe sur la Valeur Ajoutée	TVA
Netherlands	Belasting over de Toegevoegde Waarde	BTW
Portugal	Imposto sobre o Valor Acrescentado	IVA
Spain	Impuesto sobre el Valor Anadido	IVA
Sweden	Mervardeskatt	MOMS

8 ▾ Property

This chapter examines a number of situations where charities may become involved in property transactions. This includes building new premises or refurbishing and extending buildings, and situations where charities are landlords or tenants.

Generally, transactions relating to property are exempt from VAT, but there are numerous exceptions. Property transactions will often be high value and therefore of particular interest as the amount of VAT to be gained or lost is significant. Hence property transactions need to be planned with care. VAT cannot always be avoided, but each charity needs to look at the VAT consequences of various options before making a final decision on a large property transaction.

Charities generally engage in property transactions in the following ways:

▾ undertaking new construction;

▾ refurbishing and extending buildings, including listed buildings;

▾ renting out property as landlords;

▾ occupying property as tenants.

This chapter has been organised to deal with the VAT issues under these broad headings.

UNDERTAKING NEW CONSTRUCTION

Charities buying in construction services or buying a new building will either be buying in zero-rated services or standard-rated services. Construction which qualifies for zero-rating involves buildings which:

▾ are dwellings;

▾ have a relevant residential purpose;

▾ have a relevant charitable purpose.

Buildings that will be included under 'relevant residential purpose' are those where there are shared facilities. Specifically included are:

▾ children's homes;

▾ old people's homes;

82

PROPERTY

▼ homes for disabled or handicapped people;

▼ homes for the rehabilitation of persons who suffer or have suffered from:

– drug dependency;

– alcohol dependency;

– mental disorder;

▼ hospices;

▼ student living accommodation at a university, polytechnic or college (including dining rooms and kitchens if used predominantly by the living-in students);

▼ pupil living accommodation at a boarding school (including dining rooms and kitchens if used predominantly by the living-in pupils);

▼ armed forces living accommodation, such as barrack blocks and unaccompanied officers' mess quarters (married quarters are zero-rated as dwellings);

▼ living accommodation for members of religious communities;

▼ any other communal living accommodation which is the sole residence for at least 90% of the residents

'Relevant charitable purpose' means use by a charity:

▼ for the non-business activities of a charity;

▼ as a village hall or similarly in providing social or recreational facilities for a local community.

Non-business activities of charities are covered in chapter 3 *Activities of charities* (*see p22*). If the activities to take place in a building are business for the purposes of VAT, then the construction must be standard rated, even if the purchaser is a charity. There is an important distinction between activities within the charitable objects, and activities that are non-business. Business activities of charities are generally those for which the charity is paid a fee. Non-business activities are generally those which the charity undertakes voluntarily, although it may raise grants and donations to fund the work.

Confusion often arises because non-business and exempt are taken to mean the same thing. This easily happens, as the effect is similar when considering whether a charity should register for VAT; you do not register if your activities are only non-business or exempt. This is not the case with paying VAT on buildings. Exempt activities are still business activities and therefore would not qualify for the zero-rating.

For example, a private hospital which charges fees is making exempt supplies and is in business, even though it does not have to charge VAT on its fees. A charity running a hospital on donations and grants would be non-business and would be able to claim the zero-rating on new premises.

83

Note that the way in which the charity funds the construction work is not the relevant fact here; it is the purpose for which the building will be used after construction which is pertinent. A fee-paying school which raises voluntary donations to fund the construction of a new building will not qualify for the zero-rating.

The type of building makes no difference; any type of building may be a qualifying non-business charity building. This includes offices, warehouses, churches, day centres, scout or guide huts, lifeboat stations, etc. The crucial point is the non-business use.

Where there is to be minimal business use – if it is likely to be less than 10% of the total time the building is normally in use – it can be ignored. Examples of this would be where a church hires out the church hall occasionally, or a school where less than 10% of the pupils are fee-paying. Customs & Excise agreed detailed rules with effect from June 2000 on how the 10% may be calculated. It is now also possible to agree that business use is minimal by reference to floorspace or headcount, but prior approval should be obtained from the local VAT office in these instances.

Village halls and similar

The building must be owned, organised and administered by the local community for the benefit of the community. See the cases of Jubilee Hall and St Dunstan's Educational Foundation (*Summaries of useful VAT cases*), where charities tried to claim that new sports facilities were similar to village halls. It was held that the relevant conditions were only satisfied 'where a local community is the final consumer in respect of the supply of the services…in the sense that the local community is the user of the services (through a body of trustees or a management committee acting on its behalf) and in which the only economic activity is one in which they participate directly'.

However, such buildings as sports pavilions can be included if used similarly to a village hall. This will not include leisure and sports centres run by charities along commercial lines, nor swimming pools, tennis courts, bowling greens and running tracks.

Apportionment

Where only part of a building qualifies for zero-rating, then there must be an apportionment of the total contract sum. VAT at standard rate must be charged on the parts which do not qualify as relevant residential or relevant charitable use. Usually, floor area will be the basis of the apportionment and any alternative method of calculation should be cleared in advance with Customs & Excise.

Certification

In order to obtain zero-rating for certain construction work or the purchase of a new building, a certificate must be given to the contractor. There are no pre-printed forms for these certificates, but the information required is given in the example certificate at the end of this chapter (*see p92*).

Change of use

If the use of the building changes within 10 years of the completion, then VAT will have to be paid over. The change may happen either because the property is sold or the activities change in some way.

If the building is sold and will no longer have a qualifying use, then VAT should be charged on the selling price. Beware if the charity is not already registered for VAT, as this may be sufficient to cause them to register.

If there is a change of use by the same occupier, then the amount of VAT which has to be paid is the VAT saved by the zero-rating on the original construction. The date of the change of use is the effective date of a deemed supply or tax point, and VAT is due under the normal rules. Note this also applies to letting out the building, unless it can be let to a tenant which is a charity that will use it for non-business use. You can agree an apportionment if only part of the building will be used for business use.

Zero-rated works

If the building qualifies for zero-rating, the works which are generally included in the zero-rating are services supplied in the course of the construction. Included are:

▼ demolition, site clearance and earth moving;

▼ fitting of kitchen units and worktops, and kitchen appliances (but not the appliances themselves);

▼ fitting of carpets (but not the carpets themselves);

▼ domestic electrical or gas appliances designed to provide space heating or water heating or both;

▼ walls and fences;

▼ burglar and fire alarms;

▼ air conditioning;

▼ lifts and hoists;

▼ communal TV aerials;

▼ warden call systems;

▼ fitted cupboards (not elaborate fitted bedroom suites);

- bathroom fittings;
- fittings in schools such as fixed blackboards, whiteboards, gymnasium wall bars and other fixtures;
- fittings in churches such as altars, church bells, organs, fonts, lecterns, pulpits and amplification equipment.

Excluded from zero-rating are:

- architects' fees, surveyors' fees, consultants' fees or the fees of any person acting in a supervisory capacity;
- construction management services;
- site investigations;
- temporary site fencing;
- site security;
- plant hire without operator;
- kitchen appliances;
- carpets or carpeting material;
- finished or pre-fabricated furniture;
- landscaping and plants.

Design and build contracts

One supply of design and build services will be all zero-rated, provided there is one charge for the supply of construction services. Charities may wish to consider whether this is an effective way for them to buy in construction services and thereby save VAT on the professional fees.

Some charities establish a separate company in order to undertake construction work, buying in the various services from professional advisors and contractors. The company then makes one charge to the charity for the supply of construction services, which is all zero-rated. This is a legitimate method of arranging the charity's affairs as long as it is not done simply for the purpose of avoiding tax. For example, a charity may wish to ensure that liabilities ensuing from the building activity are restricted to a separate company, thus not jeopardising the charity's assets.

Long leasehold

The new construction rules apply whether the building is held freehold or leasehold, as long as the lease is for more than 21 years. Similarly, the change of use rules apply equally to the disposal of the building or part of the building by granting a long lease.

DIY building

If supporters of the charity donate their time to the charity to assist with a building project, then this may qualify as a do-it-yourself building project. Only the construction of new buildings to be used for a relevant residential or charitable purpose qualifies. The improvement or alteration of existing buildings does not qualify. Qualifying schemes allow the recovery of VAT on the materials purchased after the completion of the building on a special claim form (Form VAT 431).

REFURBISHING AND EXTENDING BUILDINGS

Generally, work done to an existing building, including any alteration, extension, reconstruction, enlargement or annexes are standard-rated. However, there are exceptions applicable to certain annexes and listed buildings.

It is sometimes difficult to determine whether the building work being undertaken should be classified as **new construction** or alteration. The difference to a charity can be significant, as there **may i** ≥ VAT at standard rate as an extra cost if the building work is judged to be alteration.

New construction work will include:

▼ demolishing an existing building to foundation level and rebuilding;

▼ demolishing all but a single wall, e.g. front façade, and then rebuilding;

▼ a separate building in the same grounds as an existing building, e.g. a new church hall with separate entrance.

Alterations include:

▼ the conversion, reconstruction, alteration or enlargement of an existing building;

▼ any extension to an existing building;

▼ rebuilding the interior of a building if the external walls were left intact even if everything else were demolished.

Annexes to charity buildings

If a charity wishes to build an annexe, it will be zero-rated, provided:

▼ the annexe is intended solely for use for a relevant charitable purpose, i.e. non-business activities;

▼ it is capable of functioning independently from the existing building;

▼ the only access (or main access where there is more than one) to the annexe is not via the existing building and vice versa.

Thus a charity annexe connected by a door or corridor to another building can be treated in the same way as a totally separate building. The annexe should be capable of functioning as intended even if the door or corridor were closed off. Therefore you should ensure that it has its own toilets, at the very least.

This does not mean that extensions or enlargements to charity buildings will qualify for zero-rating as annexes. Each case will need to be considered on its own merits, as in the case on Grace Baptist Church (*see Summaries of useful VAT cases*). You should obtain agreement from the VAT office to the zero-rating before construction commences and you may need to submit plans or allow a site visit to obtain agreement.

Listed buildings

Special rules apply to alterations to listed or protected buildings so that this work can be zero-rated in certain circumstances.

A protected building is a listed building or a scheduled monument. Unlisted buildings in conservation areas, or buildings included in a local authorities non-statutory list of buildings of local interest (Grade III buildings), are not protected buildings for the purposes of VAT.

Zero-rating will apply to 'approved alterations' on a listed building which is used for residential, relevant residential or relevant charitable purposes. This means alterations for which listed building consent is needed and has been obtained. Listed building consent is not the same as planning permission. It is a special consent needed when the proposed works will affect the character of a listed building. Therefore the construction of an extension or major improvements may require such consent. Each case is likely to be different and you will probably need the advice of an architect and to check with the local planning authority that gives the consents.

Zero-rating may include work which in other circumstances would be standard-rated as repairs and maintenance, as long as it is work directly connected to the listed building consent. Other repairs and maintenance being carried on in the building at the same time which are not covered by the listed building consent will be standard-rated. Architects' fees and the fees of any other consultants, surveyors or supervisors are standard-rated.

Fittings, furniture and carpets are standard rated as for new construction work. If the owner of the building buys any goods and materials for inclusion in the approved alteration, then they cannot be zero-rated; all goods and services must be supplied by the main contractor who zero-rates the contract sum. Certificates must be supplied to the contractor by the purchaser in the same way as the procedure for new buildings.

In the case of scheduled monuments, a similar consent has to be obtained from the Secretary of State for the Environment.

Any alteration to a church is an approved alteration provided the church is a listed building and is currently used for religious purposes.

It is important to note that buildings for business use are not eligible for the zero-rating even if they are listed buildings. The use after the approved alterations must be qualifying use by a charity or a residential use. The zero-rating will apply if a listed building is being converted into residential property.

CHARITIES AS LANDLORDS

Charities may have property as an investment or may rent out spare capacity in buildings they own for their own use.

Generally, rent will be exempt for VAT purposes. Rent on the following will always be exempt:

▼ dwellings;

▼ buildings for a relevant residential purpose;

▼ buildings for a relevant charitable purpose;

Landlords may opt to tax the rent on buildings for commercial and office use. This includes office use by charities. This makes the rent standard-rated, thus enabling the landlord to recover VAT on purchases linked to the property management. This may be advantageous where a charity landlord incurs significant maintenance and other property management costs bearing VAT, and where tenants are in a position to recover the VAT charged on the rent.

Having opted to charge VAT on rent, the option is effective for all transactions relating to the property, including a sale. The option remains effective even if the property is sold and re-acquired, and even if the owner de-registers for VAT. It may be necessary to re-register for VAT if a sale would take the organisation over the VAT threshold. The option can be revoked after 20 years.

There is some anti-avoidance legislation which does not allow the option to tax where the property will be used principally for exempt or non-business purposes and the developer is to occupy the property. This is principally targeted at financial service companies, which are partially exempt and had been establishing complex arrangements for the construction of new offices for their own occupation. This does, however, also affect many charities which also have significant exempt activities such as schools and hospitals. It will affect large-scale developments where the cost exceeds £250,000.

Service charges and other related charges

As well as charging rent, landlords will recharge some costs and service charges for additional services supplied. Generally, charges that are really part of the supply of property will be treated as falling into the same VAT category as the rent. So if the rent is exempt, then the additional charges will be exempt. Additional services that are optional or are not closely linked to the supply of property are generally standard-rated. However, if the landlord is merely acting as agent in collecting money from tenants and paying bills on their behalf, then this is outside the scope of VAT. The following are some specific situations that commonly arise.

▼ The landlord will often be the policyholder for the buildings insurance, but will recharge the cost to the tenant. This will normally be covered by a lease term and therefore fall into the same VAT category as the rent itself.

▼ Rates may be the responsibility of the landlord and recharged to tenants. Again, if this is in the lease, it will fall into the same VAT category as the rent. If the tenant is responsible for the rates, then the landlord may be acting as agent in collecting rates and paying them over on behalf of tenants.

▼ Light and power provided as part of an inclusive rental amount will not be subject to VAT where rent is exempt. A separate supply of light and power would be subject to VAT. A landlord collecting reimbursement from a tenant for a separately metered supply would be outside the scope as the landlord would be acting as an agent.

▼ Telephone lines in the name of the landlord which are then recharged to the tenants are a supply of standard-rated services.

▼ Reception services which are part of the lease agreement will fall into the same VAT category as the rent, even when charged separately. If they are an optional additional service then they will be standard-rated.

▼ Photocopying and other support services will generally be standard-rated, as charges will usually be an optional extra and charges made based on usage. If an all-inclusive rental is charged, however, then the whole amount may be exempt.

▼ Management charges by the landlord for collecting service charges and managing the property are part of the main property supply and therefore follow the VAT category of the rent.

Renting out spare capacity in charity buildings

Generally, renting out property is an exempt activity. However, there are a number of exceptions and situations where charities will need to look at this more carefully.

Rent may be exempt when a tenancy is created or a licence to occupy property is granted. This includes:

PROPERTY

▼ provision of office accommodation, such as a room or floor together with the rights to use shared areas such as reception, lifts and kitchens;

▼ provision of a specified area of office space, such as a room;

▼ provision of a serviced office, such as inclusive rent for use of telephone;

▼ hiring out a hall or other space for meetings, parties and so on, including use of kitchen, lighting, furniture and so on.

The exemption will not cover charges for a share in business services or the provision of other office services where these are provided separately. It has to be primarily a charge for the right to occupy land for the charge to be exempt. Therefore, where services such as cleaning, refreshments and staffing are provided, then this becomes a provision of a service, rather than a licence to occupy land. Hence, hiring a meeting room in a hotel will bear VAT, whereas hiring just a room can be exempt.

Hiring out sporting facilities

Short-term lets are standard-rated, but letting out facilities for more than 24 hours or a series of lettings to the same person may be exempt. This will apply to letting out a village hall for badminton as well as letting out facilities in a purpose built sports centre. A series of ten or more lettings to a school, club or association will be exempt where the same activity takes place and the activity is regular, e.g. weekly or fortnightly. The exemption can also apply if sports facilities are let out for non-sporting purposes on a regular basis, e.g. a sports hall is let out for a meeting. Sports facilities can include dance studios and any premises that have been designed or equipped specifically for a sporting or physical education purpose. Ancillary services can be included in the exemption, but this does not extend to the provision of optional extras of either equipment of staff, which should therefore be standard-rated. (*See VAT Notice 742/1 'Letting of facilities for sport and physical recreation'.*)

CHARITIES AS TENANTS

Charities often occupy premises as tenants. As charities are often in a position where they cannot recover VAT on rent charged to them, it is important to carefully consider the VAT position before entering into a lease commitment.

A landlord cannot charge VAT on rent for premises that will be used for the non-business activities of a charity ('relevant charitable purposes'). Charity offices are not included, so the office space used by a charity for its administration does not count as non-business activities for this purpose, whereas office space that is used in order to provide free counselling would be within the relevant charitable purpose. Use of part of the building as an office can be ignored if it is incidental, usually taken as less than 10% of the total floor area.

91

No certification is necessary, but charities should monitor their activities each year.

Landlords of commercial buildings have often exercised the 'option to tax', which means that the rent is subject to VAT at the standard rate. The option to tax is invalid if the premises are used for a relevant charitable purpose and so the landlord cannot charge VAT on the rent. Because of this, a landlord may refuse a tenancy to a charity, unless the charity indemnifies the landlord against losses as a result of it. The landlord will suffer a loss because he may not be able to fully recover VAT on purchases to do with the property maintenance and management where some rent is exempt. Leases should be scrutinised carefully. Hence it can be difficult for charities to find suitable premises, and renting from other charities usually presents the best option.

Sharing property

If you share a property with another charity, then care is needed when recharging services to them. If one charity is the 'lead tenant' and pays all the property bills such as rates, light and heat and then charges the other charity or charities for their share, the lead tenant is supplying services to the other charities, which are standard-rated. If all charities are tenants or joint tenants, one charity can act as an agent on behalf of the others in paying the bills. Collecting reimbursements from the other tenants is then outside the scope of VAT.

Zero-rating certificates

In order to obtain zero-rating for certain construction work or the purchase of a new building, a certification must be given to the contractor. The certificate should be accompanied with a plan of the building showing the areas eligible for zero-rating and should be produced in triplicate. The contractor needs two, as they will have to produce one to the VAT office. No certificates should be given to any sub-contractors.

The onus is on the charity or purchaser to give a correct certificate. Inspections may be made to check the use does qualify for zero-rating.

There are no pre-printed forms for these certifications, but the information required is shown opposite.

PROPERTY

Name and address of charity using the building; VAT number (*if applicable*)

Address of qualifying premises

Date or estimated date of completion of building

Estimated value of works £ . . . .

We certify that we have read the current edition of VAT Notice 708 Buildings and Construction. This certificate is being issued in respect of a supply described in that Notice at paragraph 3.3, sub-paragraph [select the appropriate clause below]:

▼ the first grant of a major interest in a relevant residential building

▼ the first grant of a major interest in a relevant charitable building

▼ the first grant of a major interest in a building converted into a relevant residential building

▼ the construction of a relevant residential building

▼ the construction of a relevant charitable building

▼ the construction of an annex to a relevant charitable building

▼ an approved alteration to a relevant residential building

▼ an approved alteration to a relevant charitable building

▼ the conversion, for a relevant housing association, of a building into a relevant residential building

We certify that the information given above is correct and complete. We are aware of the law as contained in Group 5 or Group 6 of Schedule 8 to the VAT Act 1994 and claim relief accordingly. We also certify that this organisation (in conjunction with any other organisations where applicable) is to use this building or identified parts of this building solely for a qualifying purpose. We understand that if the building or zero-rated part of it is disposed of, let or otherwise used for a non-qualifying purpose within the period of ten years from the date of its completion, a taxable supply will have been made, and this organisation (and any other organisations where applicable) will account for tax at the standard rate.

Name [print] . . . .   Position held . . . .

Signed . . . .   Date . . . .

Name and address and VAT registration of developer or building contractor:

Date certificate received by developer or builder:

Date received by VAT office:

9 ▾ Planning for VAT

This chapter looks at the areas where there is some scope for a charity to plan its activities in order to improve its VAT position, as well as giving an overview of the strategies to consider.

VAT is a complex tax, never more so than when being looked at in the context of charities. Great care must be taken in planning activities to ensure that the charity does not suddenly find itself liable for VAT, penalties and interest. Care should also be taken to look at all aspects of the planned activity, as VAT will certainly not be the only consideration. Other taxes, laws and the management structure will also affect any decisions about how activities should be organised.

There are many ways, however, in which an organisation can improve its VAT position. Some of the strategies available generally are described below. Not all of these will be suitable in all situations; in some cases the strategy requires substantial changes in your management or activities. It is not possible to cover every situation which will arise, but this should be a useful guide to some common situations.

TYPICAL VAT PROBLEMS IN CHARITIES

The main problem for most charities is that they suffer VAT on purchases that they cannot recover. Beyond the many reliefs covered in chapter 6, they will be looking for ways to recover this VAT. For this, charities need to be registered for VAT and need to see how they then maximise their VAT recovery. Usually this will involve increasing the taxable activity.

It is important to consider the VAT status of your 'customers'. If the people to whom you make charges for goods and services are able to recover VAT on purchases, then it is a lot easier to consider strategies that increase your VATable activity. You will be better off because you can charge the same price and recover VAT on your purchases, thus lowering your costs. If your customers are not registered for VAT, then it will be more difficult to simply add the VAT on top of the price you normally charge. You may have to keep your charge the same and treat this as the VAT-inclusive amount. Once the VAT is taken off the income, the net amount of income you receive may be lower.

Of course this will not be the case if you can zero rate the activity and zero-rated outputs are most efficient from the point of view of VAT planning. You really can have the best of both worlds as you do not have to charge VAT on the outputs, but you can recover the related input VAT.

Here are some common situations for charities.

▼ A charity may not have any taxable activities and therefore cannot register for VAT.

▼ A charity is about to embark on a significant expansion which will involve capital purchases and building works. It wishes to avoid or recover as much VAT as possible.

▼ A VAT-registered charity has a very low recovery rate and wishes to increase the amount of input VAT it recovers.

▼ A charity has to set up a trading subsidiary because it is starting activities which fall outside its main charitable objects. Staff costs and other costs will have to be recharged to the trading company.

▼ A charity does not want to lose income by having to account for VAT on fundraising income.

▼ A charity wants to avoid the administrative burden of VAT and considers that it would have little VAT to recover.

Charities will therefore be looking at strategies which:

▼ increase the amount of taxable supplies overall in order to achieve registration or increase the overall rate of recovery;

▼ make a particular activity taxable, rather than non-business or exempt, so that all input VAT relating to that activity may be recovered;

▼ manage activities in such a way to avoid breaching the *de minimis* limit for partial exemption, where the charity is generally below the limit;

▼ enable the charity to purchase goods without paying VAT: most of these are covered in chapter 6 *Saving VAT*;

▼ explore organisational structures which are most beneficial for VAT;

▼ avoid VAT registration where the recovery is likely to be low;

▼ plan fundraising events to maximise VAT.

In planning for VAT, you should generally arrange your affairs properly before the transactions take place. It will be very difficult to claim that the correct VAT treatment should be applied afterwards. Sometimes it is possible to backdate a claim for overpaid or under-recovered VAT, but this will be subject to the three-year 'cap'. This came into force in July 1996 and means that you can only go back three years from the date when you make the claim.

Care is also needed to think through any planning in the context of this particular area of tax law. VAT is based on European law, mainly the Sixth Directive. It is therefore different in nature to much of UK law and particularly other areas of UK tax law. The courts will look at a transaction as a whole, not necessarily the individual component parts if it has been artificially split to achieve a particular VAT effect. This was shown in the case of Card Protection Plan (*see Summaries of useful VAT cases*). In addition, the courts will ignore written contracts if they do not consider these to reflect accurately the true nature of the underlying transactions. The case of Wolverhampton Citizens' Advice Bureau (*see Summaries of useful VAT cases*) showed this.

It is also important that you can demonstrate that there were good commercial or organisational reasons for the action that you have taken. Changing the structure of the organisation or creating separate entities purely for the avoidance of tax may be challenged.

Some ideas for planning your activities from the point of view of VAT are given below. It is not an exclusive list, and all options should be considered carefully in the light of your overall position in relation to law, tax and VAT. Additional information about maximising recovery of VAT and saving VAT has been given in earlier chapters and it is worth checking these sections again. Large organisations can construct more complex schemes with the aid of professional advisors, and these are not covered here.

MEMBERSHIP SUBSCRIPTIONS

Many charities operate a membership subscription both as a means of fundraising and of building awareness of the objects of the charity. Without other evidence, one would assume that a membership subscription is standard-rated. However, some charities run membership schemes where the membership benefits are limited to voting rights and the receipt of an annual report. Customs & Excise consider that the subscription is essentially a donation in these circumstances and consequently outside the scope, or exempt in the case of professional bodies.

However, where the member receives any other benefits, the subscription will be deemed to include VAT at the full rate, unless you agree an apportionment with Customs & Excise. Values need to be attributed to the various membership benefits, by reference to cost or the price non-members pay. Then the VAT category applicable to the goods and services provided as membership benefits determine the VAT rate to apply. This must be agreed with the local VAT office in advance.

The optimum position is achieved by increasing the zero-rated element of a subscription, for example by providing publications as the chief membership benefit. Establishing the value of the publications can be achieved by putting a cover price on them, which is the amount charged to non-members. This means that all input VAT relating to membership can be recovered, whilst the output VAT is at zero rate.

ADMISSION CHARGES

Admission charges are standard-rated. If you charge for entrance to exhibitions, museums, visitors' centres or any premises or events, this would normally be standard-rated. There are, however, several ways of minimising the VAT element.

▼ If it is an event, then it may qualify as a fundraising event (*see chapter 4*). Arts organisations need to take care as an event which is the same or similar to their normal trading activities will not usually qualify as a fundraising event. Entry fees to fundraising events are exempt, although this will mean that you may not be able to recover input VAT, depending on your position on partial exemption.

▼ Keep the standard-rated element to the basic charge only and invite donations over and above the basic charge. You should not 'rig' the charges though, and the basic charge should be sufficient to cover the costs. You may decide not to charge for entrance at all and invite donations only. You must allow anyone to enter, regardless of their contribution or lack of it. Otherwise the donation is no longer truly voluntary.

▼ If you provide a printed programme on admission, then the admission charge may be apportioned to reflect the zero-rated element of the supply.

▼ Small museums, zoos, theatres, art galleries and similar may be able to treat admission fees as exempt. They must be not-for-profit bodies and managed and administered on a voluntary basis. (*See the section on Cultural services in chapter 3, p35, for more details.*)

POSTAGE AND PACKING

Books and publications are frequently supplied by mail order and many charities wish to ensure that they recover the costs of sending these out. This may cause VAT problems. Whilst you do not pay VAT when you buy stamps at the post office, the exemption is limited to supply by the Royal Mail. If you charge extra to customers for postage and packing, then you must charge VAT on that element as it is standard-rated.

If, however, you allow for the cost of postage and packing in the purchase price, then you are only making one supply, which is all related to the zero-rated publication.

GROUP REGISTRATION

Group registration is available to charitable companies and their subsidiaries. This means that one VAT return is required for the whole group and that VAT does not apply to inter-company charges.

Group registration is only available to corporate bodies, so unincorporated charities and their subsidiaries cannot have group registration. 'Corporate bodies' includes charities incorporated by royal charter or act of parliament.

A group exists for VAT purposes if one company controls another or there is common control, i.e. the same trustees. Holding a majority of the shares or voting rights, or controlling the composition of the board of directors will be taken to mean 'control'.

The advantage for charitable groups is that one group member has to be the representative member and a VAT number is issued for the group. All other VAT registration numbers for members of the group are cancelled. All supplies are treated as those of the representative member. The proportion of recoverable input VAT in the residual category will be calculated by reference to the total supplies of the whole group. For many charities, the majority of non-business activity may be in the charity and the turnover of a trading subsidiary will frequently be taxable. The charity is usually the larger entity and carries most of the overheads. Therefore the residual VAT is lying in the charity and only a small proportion can be recovered. Group registration will mean that calculations are based on the overall position of both entities taken as a whole.

The main disadvantage is that group members are jointly and severally liable for any amounts owed to Customs & Excise. It would be against the charity's objects to apply its funds to extinguish the debt of a non-charitable subsidiary. Some care is also needed to ensure that you are not using a group scheme to distort the VAT liability as Customs & Excise have powers to direct a group to remove a member in order to 'protect revenue'.

The key benefits for charity groups are:

▼ no VAT on transactions between group members;

▼ recovery of VAT calculated by reference to group turnover.

BRANCHES

If a charity has branches which are under the control of the main office, then these should be included in one registration for VAT. You have to account for their taxable supplies in the VAT return, as well as trying to gather adequate information to recover input VAT. This can be a considerable administrative burden, although it may be unavoidable if you wish to retain control over branches.

If branches are totally autonomous, however, then they do not have to be included in the main charity's VAT registration. Each branch would have to have sufficient turnover to exceed the threshold on its own, before registration would be necessary.

For this to apply, however, the branches must be completely autonomous. The constitution would have to make clear that the branch is separate and this would have to be borne out in practice. Customs & Excise look for evidence that the branch has its own management, such as an independent management committee, and is responsible for its own financial and legal affairs. A separate legal entity, such as a separate company or separate charity will normally be sufficient evidence that the entity is separately constituted.

VAT should therefore be kept in mind when structuring the charity. Your decision will depend on the size and activities of branches and what your overall VAT position is.

EDUCATION AND WELFARE ON A 'FOR-PROFIT' BASIS

Chapter 3 explores the rules applying to education and welfare services and explains that these will often fall under the exempt category of VAT. In order to be exempt, they have to be provided by an 'eligible body'. An eligible body is a not-for-profit body, providing its constitution prohibits the distribution of profits and it does not in fact distribute any profits. In addition, any profits made from exempt educational or welfare supplies, including research and vocational training, must be applied to the continuance or improvement of those activities.

A charity which wishes to increase its taxable income may wish to undertake these activities as a taxable activity. It can either channel the activity through a for-profit trading subsidiary or it can apply any profits to another activity. Clearly, you will need to consider the position of your customers in this situation. If the additional cost of the VAT you will charge on the provision of these services will be recoverable by your customers, then this will be an effective VAT planning mechanism.

FUNDRAISING EVENTS

Fundraising events organised by charities (or their subsidiaries or companies where the profits go to the charity) are exempt from VAT. This includes all the income at the event – which can be used to advantage.

▼ Banks and insurance companies wishing to sponsor your charity would have a problem in recovering any VAT charged if it is sponsorship of an on-going activity, as they are partially exempt themselves. If on the other hand they sponsor a one-off fundraising event then, as we saw in chapter 4, this income will be exempt from VAT, which will maximise the amount you will receive.

▼ Sales of standard-rated items will be exempt at a fundraising event. So sales of cassettes and adult T-shirts will be exempt, although you may charge the same price as you normally do, and so increase your income.

A PRACTICAL GUIDE TO VAT

▼ Sales of zero-rated items at a fundraising event are still zero-rated. This will apply to sales of children's clothing and auctions of donated goods. It is therefore important to keep records of income at a fundraising event so that you can retain the benefit of zero-rated supplies.

CHARGING FOR STAFF TIME AND SERVICES

There are three situations which commonly arise:

▼ a person is employed by an organisation, but the payroll is administered by another;

▼ a person is employed by one organisation, but they are seconded full-time or part-time to another organisation. In other words, there is a contract with the first organisation, but the person acts under the direction of the second organisation;

▼ a person is employed by one organisation, but undertakes some tasks for another organisation. The employee is line managed by the first organisation, their employer.

The first situation describes an agency relationship, where the employment is clearly with one organisation and payments are made on their behalf. These payments are therefore outside the scope of VAT. Any fee for the service of payroll administration would be standard-rated, however.

The second situation describes a supply of staff, which is normally standard-rated. However, supplies of staff may be outside the scope of VAT when they are not in the course or furtherance of a business. This includes secondments where no fee is paid, such as companies seconding staff to a charity. Also included in this concession are:

▼ secondments between and by government departments;

▼ secondments between National Health bodies;

▼ some secondments by and between local authorities where the activities are non-business;

▼ secondments where the employing organisation receives only reimbursement for the salary and NIC costs without making a profit, or where these amounts are paid direct to the employee and the Inland Revenue by the second organisation.

The third situation describes a supply of services, which is subject to VAT at standard rate.

However, nursing staff supplied by an agency which is acting as an agent for the hospital or institution will be treated as an exempt supply.

100

GRANTS AS A SUBSIDY FOR BUSINESS ACTIVITIES

Some organisations such as museums and galleries treat the grants they receive to support their activities as a subsidy for a business activity. Whilst no VAT is charged on the grant, since it is outside the scope of VAT, all input VAT is incurred on the business activities. Charities can establish this position if they do undertake a business activity and the grant-funded activity is not seen as a separate activity. However, it is not all that common to get this position agreed.

10 ▼ Operational aspects

This chapter looks at the practical considerations once you have registered for VAT, covering record keeping, completing VAT returns and some of the rules you need to know.

REGISTERING FOR VAT

If your taxable supplies exceed the threshold, you must complete a registration form and send it to Customs & Excise within 30 days after the end of the month. You should also register when you foresee that you will exceed the threshold within the next 30 days (*see also chapter 2 When do you have to register for VAT?*).

The date of registration is important; from that date onwards you will be expected to charge VAT. You will need time to get the VAT number and have invoices printed. Note that you may not start charging VAT before the commencement date. If the VAT number is slow to come through, then you can change your prices to reflect the VAT and then you should supply your customers with a VAT invoice after you have the registration number within 30 days of the supply.

VAT INVOICES

Once you are registered for VAT, you must issue VAT invoices for all the goods or services you supply. The only exception is where you are selling goods for cash, where there may be a *retail scheme* which you can use.

The invoice must show your name, address and VAT registration number and you should have some system for numbering invoices. It should also show the rate of VAT applicable and the amount of VAT being charged.

OPERATIONAL ASPECTS

Example: VAT invoice

A Charitable Company
North Trading Estate
Erewhon

To:

Date:

Invoice No:

Description of goods or services	
VAT @ 17.5%	
Total Due	

VAT Registration No. 12345678

TAX POINT

It is important to issue an invoice showing the correct date, known as the 'tax point'. This will normally be the date of supply, or the date of payment if it is earlier. If you supply services then the tax point will usually be the date on which the invoice is issued at the completion of the service. If you wish to ask for stage payments then you should issue an invoice and the date of issue will be the tax point. This area can be more complicated for specialised businesses. (*See VAT Notice 700 'The VAT Guide' for more detail.*)

SALES RECORDS

You must keep a copy of sales invoices you issue, which should be filed in order. In any sizeable business and where you give credit to your customers, you will probably keep a sales daybook, which is really a log of the invoices issued.

Example: Sales daybook

Invoice Number	Date	Customer	Total	VAT	Net
4026	12/7	LA of Erewhon	470.00	70.00	400.00
4027	13/7	Erewhon Social Services	235.00	35.00	200.00

PURCHASE RECORDS

A purchase daybook can be kept in a similar way for recording invoices as you receive them from suppliers. Alternatively, you may just record the payments made in your cashbook and analyse the VAT in the columns in this book.

The VAT element on all bills is separated out when the books are entered and this is the VAT which may be recovered.

Example: Cashbook payments

Date	Payee	Total	VAT	Phone	Stat'y	Equip	Audit
21/3	BT	495.76	7.38	488.38			
21/3	WH Smith	28.65	4.27		24.38		
21/3	IBM	223.24	33.25			189.99	
22/3	Simkins & Co	235.00	35.00				200.00
	Totals	982.65	79.90	488.38	24.38	189.99	200.00

A proper VAT invoice or receipt showing the supplier's VAT number must be available. It is acceptable to retain the till receipt for this purpose if the transaction amounts to less than £100, although this should still show the VAT number. For transactions above this amount, the invoice or receipt must show the rate of VAT and the amount of VAT. You must make it easy to trace bookkeeping entries back to the invoices, so that the VAT inspector can check that the correct amount of input VAT has been recovered.

COMPLETING THE VAT RETURN

When you register for VAT you will receive a VAT registration certificate and a notification of the return date. VAT returns are for a quarter, but these are not necessarily the calendar quarters. You may ask for your VAT return quarters to be aligned with your financial year.

At the end of the quarter, you need to total the VAT on sales (output tax) and the VAT on purchases (input tax).

You also need to total net sales and net purchases, excluding income outside the scope of VAT and salary costs. This information needs to be entered into the appropriate boxes on the VAT return.

You calculate the difference between output tax and input tax; if the output tax is greater, then you pay the difference to Customs & Excise. If the input tax is greater, then you will receive a payment from Customs & Excise.

You must submit returns and any payment due within a month of the quarter end.

VAT ACCOUNTING

As well as completing the VAT return, it is necessary to keep a VAT account. This is your own accounting record of your calculations to arrive at the total figures you enter on the VAT return. It should include any adjustments you have to make, such as annual adjustments, corrections of errors in previous quarters, car fuel scale charges. It should be easy to trace entries from your daybooks and cashbook. There is no particular format you have to follow for the VAT account; it is quite sufficient to show all your workings on a piece of paper which you attach to a photocopy of the VAT return in a file.

ACCOUNTING FOR VAT WHEN PARTIAL EXEMPTION APPLIES

Organisations which are registered for VAT but have substantial non-business and/or exempt activities will have complicated VAT accounting requirements. They will need to be able to identify the VAT on purchases and to relate those back to different activities by VAT category. This may necessitate more than one VAT column in the cashbook. You should ensure that you analyse the VAT into the correct column. Alternatively, you may have just one VAT column, but note by some sort of code what sort of purchase the entry is.

Example: Cashbook payments

Date	Payee	Total	VAT on taxable	VAT on exempt	VAT on non-business	VAT on shared costs
22/4	Auditor	2350.00				350.00
23/4	Printing paper	470.00	70.00			
24/4	Maintenance	235.00		35.00		
25/4	Legal fees	805.00				105.00

Many computer accounting systems will allow you to choose VAT categories and so you may be able to separate out the VAT by proper coding. The purpose of all this detail at the bookkeeping stage is to make the preparation of the VAT return easier. You will then be able to total the input VAT for taxable activities and shared costs. Apply the appropriate fraction to the input VAT on shared costs and you should be able to complete the VAT return.

This will leave you with an amount of irrecoverable VAT to transfer on a quarterly basis from the VAT account to an expense account.

RULES ON RECOVERY OF INPUT VAT

Bookkeepers need to be generally aware of the rate of VAT applying to various items which are likely to appear in petty cash claims when till receipts are often the only invoice available. Food does not generally carry VAT, but prepared food whether in a restaurant or a take away meal is standard rated. Certain items of food do carry VAT even when bought in a supermarket, for example, chocolate biscuits and fruit juice. However, it is not necessary to know the VAT rate applicable to every single item that is bought. If you do claim back some input VAT when you should not have done, then it may be found at the VAT inspection and you will be asked to repay the amount to Customs & Excise. If you regularly have to deal with some area of expenditure, then it is wise to seek advice from the local VAT office, rather than wait for a VAT inspection. It is preferable to get the advice in writing, so that you can show this to the inspector if queries arise.

MILEAGE ALLOWANCES

If mileage allowances are paid to employees, then VAT may be recovered as long as the mileage allowance only recompenses the employee for the cost of the petrol. If private mileage is reimbursed as well as business mileage, then a scale charge may have to be made. This must be looked up from a table of charges and is dependent on the size of the car and type of engine. It gives the amount of the adjustment you need to make in your VAT account by the scale charge to the output VAT.

The quarterly rates in 2000/2001 are per car:

	VAT inclusive amount	VAT amount
Diesel engine		
2,000 cc or less	£232	£34.55
over 2,000 cc	£295	£43.93
Other type of engine		
1,400 cc or less	£256	£38.12
Over 1,400 cc up to 2,000 cc	£325	£48.40
Over 2,000 cc	£478	£71.19

ACCOUNTING RECORDS

You must keep all your relevant accounting records for six years. This includes:

▼ purchase and sales books;

▼ cashbooks;

▼ petty cash books;

▼ nominal ledger;

▼ purchase invoices and copy sales invoices;

▼ purchase orders and goods received notes;

▼ records of daily takings such as till rolls;

▼ import and export documents;

▼ relevant correspondence;

▼ annual accounts;

▼ any certificates for zero-rating;

▼ workings for each VAT return;

▼ copies of VAT returns submitted.

These records should all be available for the VAT inspection. You should try to ensure that these are always up to date.

PRE-REGISTRATION PURCHASES

You may be able to recover some of the VAT incurred on purchases made before registration. These will be included on the first VAT return as input VAT. You will need to have all the VAT invoices to support the claim and it may include any goods which are still held by you. It will include services supplied in the six months before registration.

You should therefore do a stock take at the date when your VAT registration becomes effective, including stationery and equipment. You should make adjustments if you have had the equipment for a long while (equivalent to depreciation) or if you have only some of the goods left. This will be checked on your first VAT inspection.

CASH ACCOUNTING

If your taxable turnover is less than £350,000 a year, then you can use the cash accounting system. You may change to the scheme at the beginning of any VAT quarter and there is no need to tell Customs & Excise that you are doing so. There is no need to keep a sales daybook, but a cashbook for income should analyse the output VAT. The cashbook is the basis for the preparation of VAT returns.

This is advantageous for cash flow, as it means that you only pay over output VAT which you have actually collected from your customers. You must be up to date with your payments of VAT or have an agreed arrangement. You will be barred from using the scheme if you have been to court in any way in connection with VAT, or had any dishonest dealings with VAT. Care must be taken when transferring from a sales day book system to a cash accounting system that you do not double count sales and the output VAT. (*See VAT Notice 731 for full details.*)

ANNUAL ACCOUNTING

Under this scheme, the paperwork is reduced for the trader as there is only one annual return to complete. However, interim payments have to be made during the year on an estimated basis. The level and frequency of payments will depend on turnover and the amounts of VAT due. You prepare an annual return and make a final balancing payment two months after the end of the year.

You must have registered for VAT for at least a year before you can transfer to the scheme and your net taxable turnover should not exceed £300,000 per year. This scheme is not suitable if you regularly claim repayments. Your returns and payments must also be up to date before you can opt for annual accounting. You must apply for the scheme and you will receive an estimate for the monthly payments.

OPERATIONAL ASPECTS

RETAIL SCHEMES

These are ways of calculating the output VAT in situations where goods are sold for cash. This typically applies to shops. If all the sales are standard-rated, then this does not present too many problems. A record must be kept of the gross takings each day and totalled for the quarter. This is the VAT-inclusive amount, so the VAT fraction must be applied to calculate the amount of VAT included. This is:

$$\frac{\text{Standard rate of VAT}}{\text{Gross amount including VAT}} \quad \frac{17.5}{117.5} \quad \text{or} \quad \frac{7}{47}$$

So if gross takings for the day are £1,345.67, the VAT included in that amount can be calculated:

$$£1,345.67 \times \frac{7}{47} = £200.42$$

Schemes exist for shops selling a combination of standard-rated and zero-rated goods or exempt goods. For example, you may operate on a fixed profit margin, so one scheme uses the purchases as a basis for calculating the sales of standard-rate items and therefore the amount of output tax.

The scheme you choose will depend on the type of goods you sell and what your trade is; you may also suggest your own scheme if none of the existing ones are appropriate. You must obtain approval before you operate your own scheme and once you have chosen a scheme you must stay with it.

(*See VAT Notice 727.*)

BAD DEBT RELIEF

If you have customers who do not pay you, you can recover the output VAT if you have paid this over to Customs & Excise. This will not be the case for businesses on the cash accounting system. The debt should be written off in your accounts and it should be at least six months since the supply was made.

(*See VAT Notice 700/18.*)

LATE SUBMISSION OF VAT RETURN

The VAT return and the cheque for any amount due to Customs & Excise must be sent in to arrive by the due date shown. The due date is one month after the end of the VAT

109

quarter. If the return and cheque are late, then this a default. Note that you can post a return by first class post allowing one clear day for delivery and be deemed to have submitted your return on time, even if it does arrive late.

One default is not too serious and will not cost you anything, but there is an 'accumulator', so points build up for repeat offenders.

After the second default in a 12-month period, you will receive a Surcharge Liability Notice. There is nothing to pay at this stage, but a surcharge will be payable if you default again. This notice stays in effect for 12 months and during that time a surcharge is payable every time you default.

If you are late again, then you have to pay a surcharge, which is calculated as a percentage of the VAT due to be paid over. The percentage increases for each time you are late. So, the first time a surcharge is payable, it is two per cent. The second time it is payable it is five per cent, then it increases by five per cent each time you are late. There is a minimum of £30 and a maximum rate of 15%.

All late returns count as a default, but you will not have to pay a surcharge if a repayment is due. If no return is sent in, then the VAT office will assess (estimate) the VAT due and base the surcharge on that amount.

If you just do not pay VAT, Customs & Excise have powers to come to your premises and distrain (take) goods to the value of the outstanding VAT.

The VAT office will issue an assessment if the VAT return is not submitted in time. This does not absolve you from the need to send in the VAT return. The penalties can still apply.

If you are experiencing particular problems with accounting, such as a computer breakdown, then it is better to contact the VAT office and request permission to submit an estimated return, rather then just ignoring it. You can do the same in the case of illness of the person who normally prepares the return, although steps should be taken to arrange cover. It will not be acceptable to claim that no return was received, or that holidays caused a delay in its completion.

DEALING WITH CUSTOMS & EXCISE

Your first point of contact will always be the local VAT office. In some situations, the officer may need to go to the central departments dealing with particular technical areas, but you cannot get a ruling yourself from central departments.

It is always better if there is any doubt at all to enquire whether a particular activity is going to be taxable or not. There are many activities undertaken by charities which fall into 'grey areas'. Always follow up advice given over the telephone so that you get the advice in writing, as verbal advice given by a VAT officer does not help you if there is a tribunal hearing. This is particularly important if the advice is that a particular activity is not taxable and there is no need to register. Note too that advice received from an accountant will not be a valid excuse for failing to register for VAT when you should have done so. It is wise to get written confirmation from Customs & Excise in this situation as well.

A reasonable excuse may exonerate the taxpayer and penalties will then not be payable. The interpretation of reasonable excuse has been established by the courts over a period of years and the following are examples of acceptable excuses:

▼ compassionate circumstances – where a sole trader or a member of his/her immediate family is seriously ill;

▼ where a written enquiry to Customs & Excise is still outstanding concerning the status of certain activities which affects the requirements to register.

It is not acceptable to cite incompetence of an advisor or employee, nor straightforward error in the calculation.

DECLARING ERRORS

You should voluntarily disclose an error or errors as soon as possible. If the aggregate amount of errors you discover amount to less than £2,000, then these should be included in your next VAT return. No interest will be payable in this case.

If the errors in aggregate amount to more than £2,000, then this fact must be notified to Customs & Excise in writing. Interest will be payable on the overdue amount. You should not adjust your VAT return as well. If the net error is an amount repayable to you, then interest will only be calculated and remitted to you if the error arose out of misleading guidance given by a VAT officer or other Customs & Excise error.

If you do not voluntarily disclose errors when you find them, but they are discovered at the VAT visit, then it is likely that a serious misdeclaration penalty will be payable. This is calculated as 15% of the VAT misdeclared. Beware that you do not leave it too late. It is not good enough to voluntarily disclose an error when you have already been contacted to arrange a VAT visit.

For further information see leaflet 700/45.

It is considered a serious misdeclaration if you receive an assessment (because you have not submitted a VAT return) and do not inform that VAT office if it is less than the actual amount of VAT due.

These procedures do not apply to:

- ▼ annual adjustments made in the normal way for partial exemption purposes;
- ▼ returns submitted under the annual accounting scheme;
- ▼ annual adjustments made for certain retail schemes.

Note that errors and misdeclarations are considered to have lapsed if they occurred more than three years prior to discovery. The 'three-year cap' is effective for most claims whether they are in favour of the taxpayer or Customs & Excise. However, the three-year cap does not apply if there has been a deliberate attempt to evade tax.

INTEREST

Interest is payable in a number of situations involving delays in sending the correct amount of VAT to Customs & Excise:

- ▼ a VAT inspection finds mistakes in your records which mean that you have under or overclaimed VAT on returns;
- ▼ you have paid an assessment which is later found to have been too low;
- ▼ you voluntarily disclose errors which were underdeclarations or overclaims.

Generally, Customs & Excise will only pay interest to you when there have been delays in the processing of returns where a repayment was due. In those situations it is known as a 'repayment supplement' and is five per cent of the tax repayable. Interest at varying rates in line with the base rate may be due in situations where an appeal has been decided in the taxpayer's favour.

OTHER PENALTIES

There are other penalties which may be levied in other situations such as:

- ▼ certificates falsely given for zero-rating;
- ▼ proper accounting records not maintained;
- ▼ information not given to a VAT inspector;
- ▼ unauthorised issue of VAT invoices, e.g. when not registered for VAT.

Evasion of VAT is very serious indeed, although civil proceedings can be instigated instead of criminal proceedings and the penalty mitigated if you cooperate with the investigation. Proceedings will only be instigated if there is some indication that there was dishonesty involved and a deliberate intention to defraud Customs & Excise. In this situation, investigations for back-tax can be instigated for whatever time period is necessary. Where there is no fraud involved, claims are limited to a three-year period from the instigation of the claim.

OPERATIONAL ASPECTS

APPENDIX: GUIDE TO USING VAT CODING ON SAGE

If your organisation is registered for VAT and has mixed supplies of outside the scope, exempt and taxable supplies, then you need a coding structure to help you cope with the preparation of VAT returns.

The 'T' codes on Sage accounting are available to describe different rates of VAT. However, they can also be used to describe different *categories* of VAT. The categories of VAT are:

▼ outside the scope (non-business);

▼ exempt;

▼ zero-rated;

▼ standard-rated.

You will need to understand which category each activity comes into before you can operate this system. Get advice on the categories if you are unsure.

Income

It is useful to set up codes to describe each type of income. This way, you will have information about the different types of income from a VAT point of view. For example you could set up codes as follows:

▼ T0 = outside the scope income

▼ T1 = exempt income

▼ T2 = zero-rated income

▼ T3 = standard-rated income

Obviously, only the T3 coded income will then generate output VAT, which will be posted to the VAT control account. This will need to be included in the VAT return for the appropriate quarter. There will be no need to adjust this figure further.

The net income figures for exempt, zero-rated and standard-rated categories of income should be totalled and included in box 6 of the VAT return.

Purchases

You need to code all purchases for the VAT category as well. It is useful to put all the purchases that do not have any VAT on them into one code, say T4.

Then for purchases with VAT on them, you need to identify those that relate *directly* to a particular activity. For example, a conference will have direct costs and those pur-

113

chases can be identified as directly related to that activity. Use further VAT codes to attribute input VAT on costs directly attributable to a particular activity:

▼ T5 = VAT on purchases directly relating to activity outside the scope

▼ T6 = VAT on purchases directly relating to exempt activity

▼ T7 = VAT on purchases directly relating to taxable activity (both zero-rated and standard-rated)

Non-attributable VAT

You will have some costs that cannot be directly attributed to a particular area, such as the shared costs of an office. VAT on these costs should be coded to yet another code, as further work will be needed to calculate how much of this VAT is recoverable.

▼ T8 = non-attributable

You will also need to set up an expenditure heading for irrecoverable VAT and transfer the irrecoverable amount each quarter, so that it is written off as an expense.

Summaries of useful VAT cases

These are just some of the VAT cases that have particular relevance to charities. The bare facts and decision are outlined to give you an overview.

VAT cases may only have gone to the VAT Tribunal; some will go further through the courts and can go to the House of Lords or to the European Courts. The reference given will indicate which court or tribunal handled the case.

VAT cases are published in the VAT Tribunal Reports (1973–94) and the VAT and Duties Reports (from 1995) published by the Stationery Office.

The letters STC indicate that the case went to the High Court. Otherwise the reference number given is the internal reference for tribunal cases.

Apple and Pear Council 1986 (STC 192)

The Apple and Pear Development Council was set up under a statutory instrument to promote the marketing of English apples and pears. Its activities were funded by a government grant and a compulsory annual levy imposed on growers by the order. This was not held to be a business activity. It was held that the council carried out its activities not in return for the consideration from the growers but because it had a statutory obligation to do so.

Bell Concord 1989 (STC 264)

The Bell Concord Educational Trust ran the Concord College as its only activity, which was within its charitable objects of the advancement of education. It budgeted for a profit every year and so Customs & Excise challenged the 'not-for-profit' basis of its activities. A successful challenge would have meant that the college was no longer able to exempt its fees. On appeal it was held that the constitution of the organisation should be looked at to discover the purposes for which it was established, and if there was a prohibition on distributing profits then this would mean that the organisation operated 'otherwise than for a profit'.

Bowthorpe Community Trust 1995 (12978)

The trust provided training and work experience for disabled people in woodwork, pottery and other crafts. The local authority provided some funding and referred applicants for training. The trust had tried to make the connection and argue that they made a supply to the local authority and therefore should be entitled to treat it as a business supply. The tribunal found against them and held that the trust supplied training to the trainees, not to the local authority. The trust was therefore barred from recovering VAT incurred on refurbishment of the workshop premises.

British Field Sports Society 1998 (14189)

Subscription to the society entitled members to various benefits such as insurance and publications. The society had agreed an apportionment on the basis that the insurance element was exempt, the publications element was zero-rated and the balance standard-rated. They claimed back input tax on the basis of those apportionments. Customs & Excise sought to challenge the recovery of input tax on the grounds that the lobbying undertaken by the society was not a business activity. The tribunal found in favour of the society, recognising that the members joined the society because of its lobbying activities. The fact that non-members benefited from the lobbying was a necessary consequence.

Card Protection Plan 1999 (STC 199)

This case was important because it looked at the question of composite supplies and how these should be treated for VAT purposes. The company offered various services to customers for a single fee, including arranging for cash to be available and insurance cover in the event of loss or theft of credit cards, etc. The court held that the main service provided was one of convenience, with insurance as an incidental supply. This was the impression to be gathered from looking at the services as described in the company's own advertising leaflet.

Chester Zoo 1999 (STC 1027)

The North of England Zoological Society, which operates Chester Zoo, argued that its admission fees should be exempt as an educational supply. They lost in the High Court as it was ruled that the meaning of education in the VAT legislation was in its narrower meaning, in the sense of a course, a class or lesson of instruction as opposed to education in its broader sense.

The David Lewis Centre 1995 (STC 485)

This case looked at the meaning of 'relevant goods' in the context of zero-rating for medical supplies for use in diagnosis or treatment. The charity wanted the construction of soft play area for epileptic children and an observation window to be zero-rated. This was rejected because the test to be applied was a dual one, so even though it could be argued that the window might be used for the diagnosis of epilepsy, it was not a medical supply. The soft play area was excluded on both grounds.

Friends of the Ironbridge Gorge Museum 1991 (5639)

This was a separately established charity raising funds for the main charity, the museum. A subscription to the friends entitled a member to reduced entrance fees and discounts on goods in the museum shop; however, the monetary value of the benefits was very small in comparison to the amount of the subscription. Because the benefits were provided by a third party, it was held that no benefits were provided in return for the subscription and that the subscriptions were therefore outside the scope of VAT.

Glastonbury Abbey 1996 (14579)

This case concerned the definition of 'managed and administered on a voluntary basis' in the exemption applying to cultural services. UK legislation had omitted the word 'essentially' when implementing this part of the Sixth Directive and this did make a difference, the tribunal held. With only 11 paid staff, 14 trustees and 101 volunteers, the tribunal held that it was essentially managed and administered on a voluntary basis and therefore could treat admission fees to the museum as exempt. In addition, the paid staff had no financial interest in the profits from the enterprise, as they were only paid their salary.

Grace Baptist Church 1999 (16093)

This was a case where Customs & Excise challenged the zero-rating of building works, but the charity won. There was no dispute that the building was to be used for relevant charitable purpose, but customs thought the works were enlargement of an existing building, not an annexe. The tribunal held that it was an annexe, as in the ordinary dictionary meaning of a lesser building supporting a greater one. It is important to note that the existing building was demolished and a new building constructed with independent heating, fire alarm system and separately metered gas and water.

Help the Aged 1997 (STC 406)

This case was concerned with the supply of mini-buses to charities and whether these could be zero-rated. Help the Aged buys transport vans and adapts them for disabled access, selling the finished item to other charities. The case focused on two questions: whether the adaptations made the vehicles 'relevant goods' and whether the recipient charities qualified as eligible bodies. It was held that the adaptations were to last for a substantial time and that even though it was possible to put seats back into the vehicles, it was not necessary for adaptations to be irreversible for the item to come under the 'relevant goods' definition. Secondly, the recipient charities did 'care' for the individuals using the vehicles in the normal sense of the word, and there was no justification for limiting the meaning of the word 'care' to health or nursing care.

Hillingdon Legal Resource Centre 1991 (5210)

The charity provided legal advice to citizens of Hillingdon. It was funded by fees to the Legal Aid Board (taxable) and grants from the local authority and London Boroughs Grants Unit. It was claiming all input VAT back, but this was disallowed on the grounds that there was no service provided to the funding authorities, since the services provided were supplied free of charge to the users.

Jubilee Hall Recreation Centre 1999 (STC 381)

A sports centre in Covent Garden was established to provide recreation in the area of Greater London in the interest of social welfare for the benefit of the local community. In fact, the people who used the centre were people who worked in the area as well as residents and the centre was operated on a commercial basis. The centre wished to claim zero-rating for refurbishment work to the premises, which were in a listed building, on the grounds that it was used as a village hall or similar in providing social or recreational facilities for a local community and therefore qualified for relevant charitable use. It did not win the right to have the works zero-rated.

Mellerstain Trust 1989 (4256)

The tribunal held that paintings sold from an historic house open to the public were capital assets which had been used to make taxable supplies, and as such did not render the trust liable to register for VAT.

NSPCC 1992 (9325)

The NSPCC claimed that the activities of investing funds and receiving investment income were part of the business activities of the charity. The tribunal held that the mere investment of money did not in itself amount to a business activity. It further noted that the primary purpose of the charity was the charitable objects. This was in contradiction to the statement in the VAT leaflet for charities at the time, which was subsequently changed. Thus, investment income in charities should be deemed a non-business activity.

Plantiflor 2000 (STC 137)

This case looked at whether there was a single supply (of goods delivered to an address) or more than one supply. The courts decided that the particular circumstances were such that there was a supply of goods and then a supply, as agent, of a delivery service. The handling fee for the agency service was standard-rated, but the actual delivery charge was a disbursement and hence exempt. Note that it is only delivery by the Royal Mail which is exempt. Also that a disbursement will only qualify as such if the income for it is held in a suspense account.

Redrow Group plc 1999 (STC 161)

This case involved a developer who paid the estate agents' fees on the sale of their current property on behalf of people who were purchasing new houses from Redrow. The argument was put that the service was being provided to the individual purchaser, not Redrow and therefore Redrow were not entitled to recover the input VAT. In fact, Redrow won, as it was felt that Redrow had incurred the cost for the purpose of selling its houses.

RSA 1997 (STC 437)

The Royal Society for the Encouragement for the Arts, Manufacture and Commerce (RSA) sought to get a wider application of the zero-rating on charity advertising. In fact, the ruling went against them and Customs & Excise realised that they had been acting outside their powers in granting zero-rating for recruitment advertising and some other areas. Since this case it is no longer possible to convert stationery into a fundraising document and thus obtain zero-rating on those printing costs. The law was changed in April 2000 to allow zero-rating on all forms of published advertisements.

St Dunstan's Educational Foundation 1999 (STC 381)

A school with fee-paying pupils was run on land owned by a separate foundation. The foundation made the land available to the school free of charge. The foundation built a sports hall over an existing swimming pool with lottery funding. The foundation planned to allow the school free use of the facilities and local authority nominated users were to be allowed to use them for a fee. This was not allowed as non-business use, but the tribunal did consider that the sports centre was to be used as 'a village hall or similarly in providing social or recreational facilities for a local community'.

Tron Theatre 1994 (STC 177)

The theatre raised sponsorship from supporters. It claimed that part of the amount received should be a donation as the value of the sponsorship was well in excess of the real value of the benefits given in return, such as priority booking. The theatre lost. It was held that the full amount of sponsorship was the price sponsors were prepared to pay so the full amount was the consideration and therefore fully taxable.

Watford Help in the Home 1998 (15660)

This case concerned the definition of 'care'. Customs & Excise have interpreted it narrowly to mean personal services such as bathing, dressing, etc. In this case, the tribunal

A PRACTICAL GUIDE TO VAT

agreed that domestic help services such as cleaning, cooking and shopping could constitute care when supplied to 'people for whom there is either current or imminent substantial risk to the health and welfare of the person and who are unable to provide even basic self care or who have major difficulty in safely carrying out some key daily living tasks'.

Wolverhampton Citizens Advice Bureau 2000 (16411)

Wolverhampton Citizens Advice Bureau (CAB) had a service level agreement with the local authority for the provision of advice to local people. Customs & Excise won a case that argued that the CAB provided free advice that was a non-business activity, for which it received funding. Crucial to the decision was the fact that the supply was to the individual users, not to the council and therefore the council's financial support amounted to a grant.

Yoga for Health 1984 (STC 630)

This case looked at the application of the Sixth Directive and in particular Article 13A (1) (g) relating to welfare services. The charity provided therapeutic services to clients, most of whom suffered from ill-health, who paid fees and made donations to support the work of the charity. Customs argued that it was a taxable service. The charity won its appeal against the tribunal decision. The word 'welfare' connoted general physical and mental well-being and was not confined to material benefits. The language of article 13A went beyond mere material benefit and standard of living. Neither was para (g) restricted to services providing for the relief of poverty to the exclusion of services providing health care.

The Zoological Society of London 1998 (15607)

This case is similar to the Glastonbury Abbey case, but London Zoo is a much larger enterprise with 300 paid employees and a professional management team. Again, the appeal focussed on the meaning of the term 'managed and administered on a voluntary basis' in the cultural services exemption. In this case, the tribunal considered that the test needed to focus on how the *organisation* was managed, rather than how the particular activities performed by the organisation are managed. The zoo won the preliminary hearing, but the court has referred to the European Court for guidance on the interpretation of the actual words in the Sixth Directive.

Further information

Registration for VAT

Centralised at Newry VAT office. Telephone 0845 7112 114 and go through an automated answer system to leave your organisation's name and address. A form will be sent to you and you can also check progress of your application on this number. You will also be sent VAT Notice 700/1 'Should I be Registered for VAT?', which provides extensive guidance on how to complete the form.

Local VAT offices

Your local VAT office has to deal with all queries once you are registered for VAT or if you have a query about whether you should be registered. You will find the telephone number of your local VAT office by looking in the telephone directory under Customs & Excise. Call them to check whether you come within their geographical area or not. They are called 'Customs & Excise VAT Business Advice Centres'.

VAT leaflets and publications

There are various forms of publication produced by H M Customs & Excise:

▼ notices;

▼ leaflets;

▼ information sheets;

▼ guidance;

▼ business briefs.

Notices relevant to charities

700	The VAT guide
700/22	Admissions
701/1	Charities
701/5	Clubs and associations
701/6	Charity-funded equipment for medical, veterinary etc. use
701/7	VAT reliefs for people with disabilities
701/10	Liability of printed and similar matter
701/28	Lotteries
701/30	Education and vocational training
701/31	Health
701/33	Trade unions, professional bodies and learned societies
701/34	Competitions in sport and physical recreation

701/35   Youth clubs

701/41   Sponsorship

701/45   Sport and physical education

701/47   Culture

701/58   Charity advertising

706   Partial exemption

708   Buildings and construction

709/5   Tour operators' margin scheme

710/2   Agencies providing nurses and nursing auxiliaries

742/1   Letting of facilities for sport and physical recreation

CWL4   Fundraising events

Information sheets relevant to charities

8/98   Charities – supply, repair and maintenance of relevant goods
         (including adapted motor vehicles

3/99   VAT: New Deal programme

6/99   Charities: liabilities of routine domestic tasks

11/99   VAT – exemption of subscriptions to political, religious, patriotic,
         philosophical, philanthropic and civic bodies

Specific guidance relevant to charities

▼ VAT exemption of sporting services: guidance for sports clubs on the Sports Order 1999
– issued August 1999, came into effect on 1 January 2000.

Customs & Excise website

www.hmce.gov.uk

There is an extensive website, with sections on VAT and new items. In particular the website is good for checking:

▼ new guidance and information sheets;

▼ press releases;

▼ business briefs;

▼ new legislation;

▼ budget changes;

▼ latest version of leaflets and new publications.

As with many large websites, it can be difficult to find what you want, so it will not necessarily be that helpful for general enquiries.

Sayer Vincent website

www.sayervincent.co.uk

Specifically for charities and not-for-profit organisations, the Sayer Vincent website has a section on VAT, where latest news and developments are covered as well as detailed guidance aspects of VAT relevant to charities. It also has sections on other areas of financial management and fundraising for charities.

Books and reference texts on VAT

Tolley's Value Added Tax, updated annually after the Finance Bill. Aimed at practising accountants, this is a technical guide which covers all the main areas, referenced to the legislation and VAT notices. It is published by Butterworths Tolley, 2 Addiscombe Road, Croydon, Surrey, CR9 5AF. Tel: 020 8686 9141

Other law and guidance

The Voluntary Sector Legal Handbook, 2nd edition 2001, Sandy Adirondack and James Sinclair Taylor, Directory of Social Change

This covers employment law, constitutional issues and many other areas. Use to check the fundraising regulations under the Charities Act 1993, the law and regulations relating to lotteries.

The Fundraiser's Guide to the Law, 1st edition 2000, Bates, Wells & Braithwaite and Centre for Voluntary Sector Development, Directory of Social Change in association with Charities Aid Foundation

This gives information on the law as it relates to large-and small-scale fundraising activities. Structured according to fundraising activity, it provides advice on key topics such as contracts, insurance, VAT, data protection and tax – including details of changes in 2000.

Index

accounting records 105, 107

acquisitions 78

acupuncturists 30

admission charges 34, 35–6, 38, 43, 97

advertisements, fundraising 40, 44, 63, 73

advertising space, selling 38, 43, 47

affinity credit cards 42

aids for disabled people 37, 64–5, 78–9

alarm systems 68

ambulances 65

annexes to charity buildings 87–8

annual accounting 108

annual adjustment 54–5, 60

Apple and Pear Council 24, 115

apportionment: of income 13

of membership benefits 25, 26, 33, 34

of residual VAT 50, 51, 57–9

art exhibitions 25, 35, 97

art galleries 25, 35, 36, 97, 101

arts organisations 25, 97

auctions, charity 46, 100

bad debt relief 109

badges 23, 40, 66

bail hostels 31

barter arrangements 47, 48

Bell Concord 31, 115

bingo 45

boats for disabled people 66

books 8, 17, 36, 37, 45, 71, 72, 97

Bowthorpe Community Trust 24, 115–16

branches 17–18, 98–9

British Field Sports Society 116

buildings:

alterations/conversions/extensions 68, 74, 87–9

change of use 85

construction 36, 67, 82–7, 92–3

listed/protected 37, 88–9

renting/renting out 89–92

business activities 8, 9, 21, 22

cancelling registration 15, 18–19, 80

Card Protection Plan 96, 116

cards *see* printed matter

care services 31, 32, 119–20

cash accounting 108

cassette players 72, 73

cassettes 37, 38, 71, 99

catering 34, 38

cause-related marketing 41

CD-ROMs 37, 38

certificates, zero-rating:

advertising 73–4

buildings 74, 85, 92–3

disabled access 74

challenge events 43–4

Chester Zoo 116

Christmas cards 42, 46

clothing and footwear 8, 37, 65, 77, 100

coding invoices 57, 105–6

coffee mornings 43

collecting tins 40, 66

collections 39, 40

colleges 28, 115

'commercial influence' 33

conferences 28, 66–7

'consideration' 8

consultancy services 29, 30, 38

contracts 24, 25

with TECs 29

corporate donations 40–1

124

corporate events 41–2

cultural services 35–6

Customs & Excise, dealing with 110–11

daycentres 68, 70, 84

de minimis limits 51, 52, 53

dental services 30, 65

de-registration 18–20

design and build contracts 86

direct mail 40, 63, 67–8

disabled people: access 68, 74

   see also aids

distance selling 79–80

dividends 23

DIY building 87

domestic help 31, 119–20

donations 22, 23, 39, 40

education 22, 27–30, 99, 115

'eligible bodies': cultural 35–6

   education 28, 99

   sports exemption 33, 34

entry fees *see* admission charges

envelope collections 40, 66

errors, declaring 111–12

events *see* fundraising events

examination fees 30

exempt activities 9, 12, 20, 21, 26–30, 56, 83

exemption from registration 17

exhibitions 25, 35, 97

exports 37, 75, 76

food 8, 36, 77, 106

'Friends of...' organisations 18

Friends of the Ironbridge Gorge Museum 117

fuel and power 62, 69

fully taxable status 51–2

fun runs 43

funding agreements 23–4

fundraising events 42–3, 63, 97, 99–100

   corporate 41–2

galleries 25, 35–6, 97, 101

gifts in kind 47

Glastonbury Abbey 36, 117

Grace Baptist Church 88, 117

grants 22–5, 39

   as subsidies 24, 25, 101

group registration 38, 97–8

health care 30, 31, 32

hearing aids 65, 69

Help the Aged 117

Hillingdon Legal Resources Centre 118

home help services 31, 119–20

homes, care 31, 32, 68, 82, 83

   medical equipment 69–70

hospitals 64, 83, 89

   medical equipment 69–70

   trolleys 32

house alteration *see* buildings

imports 37, 69, 77

input VAT 9, 10, 49, 50, 106

interest: bank 23

   on late payment 112

international services 37, 75–6

Internet 37, 63

investment income 23

invoices, VAT 102–4

   coding 57, 105–6

Jubilee Hall Recreation Centre 84, 118

jumble sales 43

lapel badges *see* badges

late registration 15–16

late submission of returns 109–10

leaflets *see* printed matter

leasehold properties 86

legacies 23

Legal Aid Board funding 24

Lewis (David) Centre 116

life subscriptions 26

lifeboats 69

listed buildings 88–9

lotteries 44–5, 63

meals on wheels 22

medical equipment 64, 69–70, 77

medicines 37, 70, 77

Mellerstain Trust 118

membership subscriptions *see* subscriptions

merchandising 47

mileage allowances 106–7

Motability scheme 70

museums 25, 35–6, 97, 101, 117

New Deal 29

non-business activities 9, 22–3, 56, 83

NSPCC 118

nurseries 32

nursing staff 30, 32, 62, 70, 100

osteopaths 30

output VAT 9, 10

'outside the scope' 8, 9, 12, 22–3

overseas subscriptions 26

partial exemption 51–7, 105–6

penalties 74, 110, 111, 112–13

   for late registration 15–16

   serious misdeclaration 111, 112

photocopying 38, 71, 90

physical recreation *see* sport

Plantiflor 118–19

playgroups 32

political parties: subscriptions 25, 32–3

postage and packing charges 38, 97

power supplies 69

pre-registration purchases 15, 108

printed matter 8, 17, 34, 37, 61, 63, 71–2

probation hostels 31

professional bodies: subscriptions 25, 32–3

property *see* buildings

provisional recovery rate 60

publications 17, 96, 97

purchase records 104

radios 36, 72, 73

raffles 44–5, 46

recharges: property costs 90, 92

   staff time and services 100

records, keeping 104, 105, 107

recruitment advertisements 63, 119

Redrow Group plc 119

reduced-rate 9

reflexologists 30

registration, VAT 7, 12–16, 19–20, 75, 79, 80,
   102

religious organisations 25

renting out property 89–91

renting out sports facilities 35, 91

renting property 91–2

rescue equipment 72

research 30, 99

residual input VAT 50

   apportionment of 50, 51, 57–9

retail schemes 102, 109

returns, VAT 105

royalties 38

RSA 119

Sage accounting 113–14

St Dunstan's Educational Foundation 84, 119

sale of donated goods 37, 39, 45–6, 99–100

sales records 104

schools 22, 28, 30, 84, 89, 119

secondment of staff 23, 76, 100

service charges, property 90, 92

services: and contracts and grants 24, 25

    free 22, 24

    international 76–7

    to other charities 47

share dealing 23

shops 45, 46

Sixth Directive, EC 35, 36, 96

societies: subscriptions 25, 32–3

spectacles 30, 65, 73

sponsorship 40–1, 43–4, 99

sport 27, 33

sports club subscriptions 25, 34

sports competitions 34

sports facilities 34, 35, 84, 91

staff secondments 23, 100

standard-rated 9, 38

stationery *see* printed matter

subscriptions 23, 25–6, 32–3, 34, 37, 96–7

'supplies' 8, 12

    made below cost 22

Surcharge Liability Notices 110

talking books 36, 72

tape players/recorders 72, 73

tax point 103

taxable activities 8, 9, 12, 13, 21, 94, 95

telephone fundraising 40

telesales 63

theatres 41, 97, 119

threshold, registration 12, 13, 14

Tour Operator's Margin Scheme (TOMS) 43–4

trade union subscriptions 25, 32–3

trade within EC 78–81

Trader's Unique Reference Number (TURN) 77

trading subsidiaries 18, 38, 42, 63, 95, 97, 98, 99

training courses 28–9, 66–7

transport services 34, 37

Tron Theatre 41, 119

universities 28

vehicles 64, 65, 70, 72–3

videos 37, 38, 69, 71

village halls 35, 83, 84

visual aids 30, 65, 73

vocational training 28–9, 67, 99

voluntary registration 14–15, 80

voluntary services 22

Watford Help in the Home 31, 119–20

welfare services 32, 31, 99

wireless sets 36, 72, 73

Wolverhampton Citizens Advice Bureau 24, 96, 120

work placement schemes 23

Yoga for Health 120

youth clubs 29

zero-rated 9, 20, 36–7, 61, 83–4, 94

    see certificates, zero-rating

Zoological Society of London 36, 120

zoos 25, 35, 36, 97, 116, 120